THE
HIDATSA

THE
HIDATSA

Mary Jane Schneider
University of North Dakota

Frank W. Porter III
General Editor

CHELSEA HOUSE PUBLISHERS
New York   Philadelphia

On the cover Hidatsa saddlebag made of tanned hide and trimmed with metal, beads, and dyed horsehair.

Chelsea House Publishers
Editor-in-Chief Nancy Toff
Executive Editor Remmel T. Nunn
Managing Editor Karyn Gullen Browne
Copy Chief Juliann Barbato
Picture Editor Adrian G. Allen
Manufacturing Manager Gerald Levine

Indians of North America
Senior Editor Marjorie P. K. Weiser

Staff for **THE HIDATSA**
Assistant Editor Karen Schimmel
Copy Editor Karen Hammonds
Deputy Copy Chief Ellen Scordato
Editorial Assistant Tara P. Deal
Assistant Art Director Laurie Jewell
Senior Designer Victoria Tomaselli
Picture Researcher Villette Harris
Production Coordinator Joseph Romano

First Printing

1 3 5 7 9 8 6 4 2

Library of Congress Cataloging in Publication Data

Schneider, Mary Jane.
The Hidatsa / Mary Jane Schneider; Frank W. Porter, editor.
   p.   cm. — (Indians of North America)
Bibliography: p.
Includes index.
ISBN 1-55546-707-5
1. Hidatsa Indians. I. Porter, Frank W., 1947– .
II. Title. III. Series: Indians of North America (Chelsea
House Publishers)   88-11702
E99.H6S36 1989   CIP
970.004'97—dc 19   AC

CONTENTS

INDIANS OF NORTH AMERICA

CHELSEA HOUSE PUBLISHERS

INDIANS OF NORTH AMERICA: CONFLICT AND SURVIVAL

Frank W. Porter III

The Indians survived our open intention of wiping them out, and since the tide turned they have even weathered our good intentions toward them, which can be much more deadly.

John Steinbeck
America and Americans

When Europeans first reached the North American continent, they found hundreds of tribes occupying a vast and rich country. The newcomers quickly recognized the wealth of natural resources. They were not, however, so quick or willing to recognize the spiritual, cultural, and intellectual riches of the people they called Indians.

The Indians of North America examines the problems that develop when people with different cultures come together. For American Indians, the consequences of their interaction with non-Indian people have been both productive and tragic. The Europeans believed they had "discovered" a "New World," but their religious bigotry, cultural bias, and materialistic world view kept them from appreciating and understanding the people who lived in it. All too often they attempted to change the way of life of the indigenous people. The Spanish conquistadores wanted the Indians as a source of labor. The Christian missionaries, many of whom were English, viewed them as potential converts. French traders and trappers used the Indians as a means to obtain pelts. As Francis Parkman, the 19th-century historian, stated, "Spanish civilization crushed the Indian; English civilization scorned and neglected him; French civilization embraced and cherished him."

Nearly 500 years later, many people think of American Indians as curious vestiges of a distant past, waging a futile war to survive in a Space Age society. Even today, our understanding of the history and culture of American Indians is too often derived from unsympathetic, culturally biased, and inaccurate reports. The American Indian, described and portrayed in thousands of movies, television programs, books, articles, and government studies, has either been raised to the status of the "noble savage" or disparaged as the "wild Indian" who resisted the westward expansion of the American frontier.

7

Where in this popular view are the real Indians, the human beings and communities whose ancestors can be traced back to ice-age hunters? Where are the creative and indomitable people whose sophisticated technologies used the natural resources to ensure their survival, whose military skill might even have prevented European settlement of North America if not for devastating epidemics and the disruption of the ecology? Where are the men and women who are today diligently struggling to assert their legal rights and express once again the value of their heritage?

The various Indian tribes of North America, like people everywhere, have a history that includes population expansion, adaptation to a range of regional environments, trade across wide networks, internal strife, and warfare. This was the reality. Europeans justified their conquests, however, by creating a mythical image of the New World and its native people. In this myth, the New World was a virgin land, waiting for the Europeans. The arrival of Christopher Columbus ended a timeless primitiveness for the original inhabitants.

Also part of this myth was the debate over the origins of the American Indians. Fantastic and diverse answers were proposed by the early explorers, missionaries, and settlers. Some thought that the Indians were descended from the Ten Lost Tribes of Israel, others that they were descended from inhabitants of the lost continent of Atlantis. One writer suggested that the Indians had reached North America in another Noah's ark.

A later myth, perpetrated by many historians, focused on the relentless persecution during the past five centuries until only a scattering of these "primitive" people remained to be herded onto reservations. This view fails to chronicle the overt and covert ways in which the Indians successfully coped with the intruders.

All of these myths presented one-sided interpretations that ignored the complexity of European and American events and policies. All left serious questions unanswered. What were the origins of the American Indians? Where did they come from? How and when did they get to the New World? What was their life—their culture—really like?

In the late 1800s, anthropologists and archaeologists in the Smithsonian Institution's newly created Bureau of American Ethnology in Washington, D. C., began to study scientifically the history and culture of the Indians of North America. They were motivated by an honest belief that the Indians were on the verge of extinction and that along with them would vanish their languages, religious beliefs, technology, myths, and legends. These men and women went out to visit, study, and record data from as many Indian communities as possible before this information was forever lost.

8

By this time there was a new myth in the national consciousness. American Indians existed as figures in the American past. They had performed a historical mission. They had challenged white settlers who trekked across the continent. Once conquered, however, they were supposed to accept graciously the way of life of their conquerors.

The reality again was different. American Indians resisted both actively and passively. They refused to lose their unique identity, to be assimilated into white society. Many whites viewed the Indians not only as members of a conquered nation but also as "inferior" and "unequal." The rights of the Indians could be expanded, contracted, or modified as the conquerors saw fit. In every generation, white society asked itself what to do with the American Indians. Their answers have resulted in the twists and turns of federal Indian policy.

There were two general approaches. One way was to raise the Indians to a "higher level" by "civilizing" them. Zealous missionaries considered it their Christian duty to elevate the Indian through conversion and scanty education. The other approach was to ignore the Indians until they disappeared under pressure from the ever-expanding white society. The myth of the "vanishing Indian" gave stronger support to the latter option, helping to justify the taking of the Indians' land.

Prior to the end of the 18th century, there was no national policy on Indians simply because the American nation had not yet come into existence. American Indians similarly did not possess a political or social unity with which to confront the various Europeans. They were not homogeneous. Rather, they were loosely formed bands and tribes, speaking nearly 300 languages and thousands of dialects. The collective identity felt by Indians today is a result of their common experiences of defeat and/or mistreatment at the hands of whites.

During the colonial period, the British crown did not have a coordinated policy toward the Indians of North America. Specific tribes (most notably the Iroquois and the Cherokee) became military and political pawns used by both the crown and the individual colonies. The success of the American Revolution brought no immediate change. When the United States acquired new territory from France and Mexico in the early 19th century, the federal government wanted to open this land to settlement by homesteaders. But the Indian tribes that lived on this land had signed treaties with European governments assuring their title to the land. Now the United States assumed legal responsibility for honoring these treaties.

At first, President Thomas Jefferson believed that the Louisiana Purchase contained sufficient land for both the Indians and the white population.

Within a generation, though, it became clear that the Indians would not be allowed to remain. In the 1830s the federal government began to coerce the eastern tribes to sign treaties agreeing to relinquish their ancestral land and move west of the Mississippi River. Whenever these negotiations failed, President Andrew Jackson used the military to remove the Indians. The southeastern tribes, promised food and transportation during their removal to the West, were instead forced to walk the "Trail of Tears." More than 4,000 men, women, and children died during this forced march. The "removal policy" was successful in opening the land to homesteaders, but it created enormous hardships for the Indians.

By 1871 most of the tribes in the United States had signed treaties ceding most or all of their ancestral land in exchange for reservations and welfare. The treaty terms were intended to bind both parties for all time. But in the General Allotment Act of 1887, the federal government changed its policy again. Now the goal was to make tribal members into individual landowners and farmers, encouraging their absorption into white society. This policy was advantageous to whites who were eager to acquire Indian land, but it proved disastrous for the Indians. One hundred thirty-eight million acres of reservation land were subdivided into tracts of 160, 80, or as little as 40 acres, and allotted to tribe members on an individual basis. Land owned in this way was said to have "trust status" and could not be sold. But the surplus land—all Indian land not allotted to individuals— was opened (for sale) to white settlers. Ultimately, more than 90 million acres of land were taken from the Indians by legal and illegal means.

The resulting loss of land was a catastrophe for the Indians. It was necessary to make it illegal for Indians to sell their land to non-Indians. The Indian Reorganization Act of 1934 officially ended the allotment period. Tribes that voted to accept the provisions of this act were reorganized, and an effort was made to purchase land within preexisting reservations to restore an adequate land base.

Ten years later, in 1944, federal Indian policy again shifted. Now the federal government wanted to get out of the "Indian business." In 1953 an act of Congress named specific tribes whose trust status was to be ended "at the earliest possible time." This new law enabled the United States to end unilaterally, whether the Indians wished it or not, the special status that protected the land in Indian tribal reservations. In the 1950s federal Indian policy was to transfer federal responsibility and jurisdiction to state governments, encourage the physical relocation of Indian peoples from reservations to urban areas, and hasten the termination, or extinction, of tribes.

Between 1954 and 1962 Congress passed specific laws authorizing the termination of more than 100 tribal groups. The stated purpose of the termination policy was to ensure the full and complete integration of Indians into American society. However, there is a less benign way to interpret this legislation. Even as termination was being discussed in Congress, 133 separate bills were introduced to permit the transfer of trust land ownership from Indians to non-Indians.

With the Johnson administration in the 1960s the federal government began to reject termination. In the 1970s yet another Indian policy emerged. Known as "self-determination," it favored keeping the protective role of the federal government while increasing tribal participation in, and control of, important areas of local government. In 1983 President Reagan, in a policy statement on Indian affairs, restated the unique "government to government" relationship of the United States with the Indians. However, federal programs since then have moved toward transferring Indian affairs to individual states, which have long desired to gain control of Indian land and resources.

As long as American Indians retain power, land, and resources that are coveted by the states and the federal government, there will continue to be a "clash of cultures," and the issues will be contested in the courts, Congress, the White House, and even in the international human rights community. To give all Americans a greater comprehension of the issues and conflicts involving American Indians today is a major goal of this series. These issues are not easily understood, nor can these conflicts be readily resolved. The study of North American Indian history and culture is a necessary and important step toward that comprehension. All Americans must learn the history of the relations between the Indians and the federal government, recognize the unique legal status of the Indians, and understand the heritage and cultures of the Indians of North America.

"The Eagle Catcher" by Edward S. Curtis. Many of this photographer's pictures of the Hidatsa were published in 1909 in volume IV of The North American Indian, *a 20-volume series completed in 1930.*

THE PEOPLE
OF
THE WILLOWS

[Their] three villages . . . [are] on the banks of Knife river; a small stream, so called, meandering through a beautiful and extensive prairie, and uniting its waters with the Missouri. . . . The principal village. . . . contains forty or fifty earth-covered wigwams, from forty to fifty feet in diameter, and being elevated, overlooks the other two, which are on lower ground and almost lost amidst their numerous corn fields and other profuse vegetation which cover the earth with their luxuriant growth. . . .

[The people] are generally tall and heavily built. . . . I have happened to visit them in the season of their festivities, which annually take place when the ears of corn are of the proper size for eating. The green corn is considered a great luxury by all those tribes who cultivate it; and is ready for eating as soon as the ear is of full size, and the kernels are expanded to their full growth, but are yet soft and pulpy. In this green state of the corn, it is boiled and dealt out in great profusion to the whole tribe, who feast and surfeit upon it whilst it lasts; rendering thanks to the *Great Spirit* for the return of this joyful season, which they do by making sacrifices, by dancing, and singing songs of thanksgiving. . . .

The scenes described by artist George Catlin in 1832 probably differed little from those viewed by the first non-Indian visitors to the Great Plains. In 1541 a small band of Spanish explorers led by Francisco Vásquez de Coronado had marched into the territory that is now the southwestern United States. They became the first Europeans to explore the Plains, the grassy highlands that cover the center of North America. The reports of the expedition describe a "sea of grass" so flat and empty that men got lost and buffalo as numerous as "fish in the sea." These explorers were the first outsiders to come upon the Indians of the Plains. Their reports contain the earliest descriptions of Plains Indian life. Some of the tribes met by the Spanish moved from place to place,

The Hidatsa Green Corn Dance, a celebration of thanksgiving for the new crop of corn, painted by George Catlin about 1835.

following and hunting the buffalo herds. Others were farmers, living in villages of grass-covered houses and cultivating fields of corn, squash, and beans. Because the flat, grassy terrain of the Plains was similar to their homeland, the Spanish were particularly impressed with the fertility of the land.

Later explorers and travelers who crossed the Great Plains were not so impressed. They found the desertlike heat, constant wind, and limitless grasslands so fearsome that the region became known as the great American desert. Nineteenth-century American

scholars concluded that humans could not survive there without horses and guns. These scholars reasoned that if people needed horses and guns, then the Plains Indians, like the Euro-Americans, must be newcomers to the region. This thinking underestimated the antiquity and ability of the Plains Indians. Today we know that the way of life described by Coronado's expedition represented thousands of years of adjustment to the resources and hazards of the Plains.

Among the Indians living on the Great Plains at that time was the tribe now known as Hidatsa, the People of the Willows. Originally Hidatsa had been the name of a small group of people living on the Missouri River in what is now western North Dakota. Two related groups were nearby: the Awatixa (Ah-WAH-ti-HA), or People of Rock Village, and the Awaxawi (Ah-WAH-ha-WEE), or People of Mountain Village. These three groups would one day come together to form the Hidatsa tribe. Although the Hidatsa, Awatixa, and Awaxawi spoke similar languages, each village had its own history and government. The people did not think of themselves as members of a common tribe.

Not far from these villages, on the opposite bank of the Missouri River, lived the Mandan. The Mandan called the Hidatsa *Minitari*, which means "cross the water." Early non-Indian visitors sometimes referred to the Hidatsa by this name. French traders called the Hidatsa the *Gros Ventres*, or Big Bellies. This is the name that usually appears on treaties and other legal documents between representatives of the tribe and various countries.

The Hidatsa and Mandan had similar ways of life, or cultures. Like other Plains Indians, they hunted buffalo and a variety of other animals and gathered wild plant foods from the environment. The Plains tribes depended on the buffalo, also called the bison, to provide them with many necessities of life— meat for food, hides for clothing and shelter, bones for utensils, needles, and decoration, among other uses. Some

Plains tribes obtained all of their food by hunting and gathering. These people lived as nomads, following the buffalo herds as they moved from place to place. Other Plains tribes supplemented their diet of meat and foods that they gathered by growing corn, beans, and squash. These people built permanent villages and hunted buffalo only when the huge animals could be found in their hunting territory.

Both the Hidatsa and the Mandan were among the settled Plains tribes. They lived in permanent villages and practiced horticulture (farming with simple hand tools). Because they lived near each other and had similar cultures, the two tribes were frequent allies. Consequently, they are often mentioned together in written accounts by explorers, traders, and other non-Indians.

Although buffalo hunting and horticulture were both ancient ways of surviving in the Plains environment, buffalo hunting was older. Archaeologists have studied the stone spear points and other kinds of evidence found when ancient campsites and village sites have been excavated. As a result, they have established some general stages in the development of the Plains Indians' way of life.

The earliest stage or most ancient way of life is that of the Paleo-Indian period. Most archaeologists and geologists believe that the first people in North America came from Asia sometime between 25,000 and 14,000 years ago. At one time much of North America was covered by glaciers (huge sheets of snow and ice), and the sea levels were lower than they are today. At that time a land bridge, an open, tundralike plain now referred to as Beringia, connected Asia to what is now Alaska. Giant bison, moose, deer, and other large animals probably traveled across Beringia and entered North America. Archaeologists believe that the first North Americans, whom they call Paleo-Indians, were hunters from northern Asia who followed the big animals across Beringia. Although archaeologists do not know exactly when the first migrations occurred, they do know that at some time before 12,000 B.P. (before the present) the Paleo-Indians were well established in several locations throughout the continent, including the Plains.

North America at that time was wetter and cooler than it is today. The areas that were not covered with glaciers

Spanish explorers were the first non-Indians to view the American bison, popularly known as the buffalo. This 16th-century woodcut, reproduced from a drawing by an unknown artist, was probably based on descriptions found in the writings of early Spanish explorers. It is believed to be the first picture of a buffalo seen in Europe.

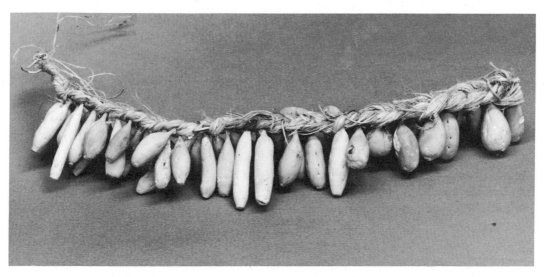

Prairie turnips, an important source of food for the Plains Indians, were dried and stored after their stems were braided together.

were covered with forests. Regions that today are dry were then lush grasslands. Gradually, over many centuries, the climate warmed and the glaciers began to melt. Huge lakes and rivers formed by the melting ice provided water for the remarkable animals that inhabited this new world. Beavers as large as bears and buffalo with horn spreads of six feet could be found. In addition, mammoths (hairy, elephant-like creatures) and mastodons (a relative of the mammoth) as well as camels and other animals that are now extinct in North America flourished there in ancient times.

The earliest Paleo-Indian sites uncovered by archaeologists are places where mammoths were killed. The first site at which stone weapon tips called projectile points were found together with the bones of a hunted mammoth

was near Clovis, New Mexico. Consequently, the culture of the people that inhabited the area is called Clovis, and the distinctive, grooved projectile points are called Clovis points. Some archaeologists believe that there were older cultures in North America, but because Clovis-type points have been found over a wide area, the Clovis culture is so well known that most people use it to mark the beginning of human life on this continent.

In order to kill an animal as big as a mammoth, the Clovis people must have been intelligent and skillful hunters. Archaeologists believe the Clovis points were bound to slender wood shafts to make throwing spears. To kill a mammoth, the Clovis hunters may have first trapped the animal in a swampy area and then weakened it by throwing spears at it. Finally, after the mammoth

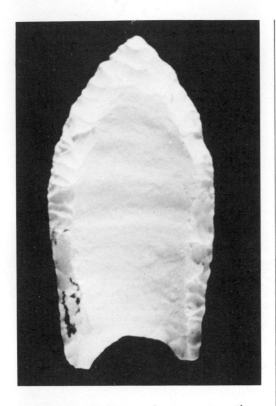

Based on the discovery of stone weapon tips, such as this Folsom point, in western North Dakota, archaeologists have determined that Paleo-Indians visited the area thousands of years ago.

was weakened by fighting and loss of blood, the hunter could approach and stab it in a vital organ. In addition to hunting mammoths, the Clovis people hunted giant buffalos, camels, horses, tapirs (large, long-snouted, chiefly nocturnal animals), and smaller animals.

The Clovis people made a variety of stone and bone tools that they used for different tasks. Some tools were used to butcher the animals they killed; others appear to have been used to prepare the animals' hides. The Clovis people probably made tents and clothing out of hides, but these articles have not been found by archaeologists. Grinding stones have been found, suggesting that the Clovis people collected nuts or seeds and ground them to a fine meal for food.

Most of the region that is now North Dakota was covered with ice 300 to 1,000 feet thick during the Paleo-Indian period. Only that area of the state that was west of the Missouri River—which would later become the Hidatsa's homeland—was not covered with ice. Today that area is rugged terrain. Central North Dakota, which was scoured and flattened by the melting glaciers, is now gently rolling grassland. The huge lakes formed when the glaciers melted eventually became rivers, marshes, and small, shallow waterholes. No Paleo-Indian hunting or camping sites have been uncovered in North Dakota, but a number of Clovis points found there indicate that these early hunters were in the region. Some of the points found here are made of a distinctive North Dakota brown flint stone called Knife River flint.

Around 11,000 years ago the climate of North America became warmer and drier. In the center of the continent, grasslands replaced what were once forests. Many of the large animals disappeared. Some scientists think the animals died out because they could not adjust to the changes in the environment caused by the drier climate. Others think the Clovis people may have killed too many of them, leading to their becoming extinct. As the environment changed, the size of the buffalo also changed. A smaller strain of buffalo evolved that was more suited to finding food in the new environment. The later Paleo-Indians hunted this animal.

These later hunters belong to what is known as the Folsom culture, after the site at Folsom, New Mexico, where the first evidence of their existence was found. The Folsom people hunted the smaller buffalo by driving them over cliffs or trapping them in canyons. Archaeologists have studied massive piles of butchered buffalo bones found at the sites where the animals were killed. They have determined that the carcasses were first cut into large chunks containing the meat preferred by the Folsom people. Gristle and tough cuts were often left behind, and the tender meat was carried away to be cut into smaller portions. The Folsom people also hunted other animals and collected wild plant foods. They made tools from stone and bone. These materials were also made into beads, which the Folsom people used to decorate themselves and their clothing.

Evidence from the Lindenmeier site, a Folsom location in Colorado, suggests that the Folsom people lived in small groups of 15 to 20 people. These groups were involved in trade networks that exchanged obsidian (volcanic glass), which could be found only in certain areas, and the best types of flint stone from different parts of the country. Although little is known about the Folsom people, it is evident that they were skilled hunters who developed hunting and butchering techniques that continued to be used by American Indians into the 20th century.

By about 10,000 B.P., ways of life in North America had become more var-

Until Europeans introduced metal implements, Indians made their tools from materials they found in the environment. This buffalo-bone tool, used in catching eagles, anchored a stuffed rabbit skin to a branch. The rabbit served as a decoy to lure a bird close enough to be caught with human hands.

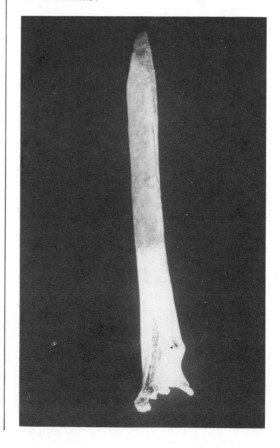

ied. At archaeological sites of this late Paleo-Indian period, the grooved spear points of earlier times are found less frequently, and several different types of points start to show up. These new points have edges that were carefully shaped on both sides by flaking, or removing small chips of stone. Archaeologists have identified four variations in the way of life of the late Paleo-Indians. These cultures are named for important sites where their artifacts have been found—Hell Gap Agate Basin, Cody, Plainview—or for the way in which stone was chipped to make the tool—Parallel Oblique Flaked, for example. Spear points of all these groups have been found in western North Dakota. The different types of points show an increasing awareness and use of local environments. The differences from one place to another eventually resulted in the unique tribal cultures of recent times. Thus the varied groups of these early days connect Paleo-Indians to later Indian cultures.

The climate continued to be dry, and by about 8,000 years ago the Great Plains region had become much like it is today. By then the buffalo had at-

Stone spear points found by archaeologists in different areas on the Plains represent four distinct late Paleo-Indian cultures. (left to right) Parallel Oblique Flaked, Cody, Plainview, and Hell Gap Agate Basin.

tained its present size. The people were now making use of more of the local plant and animal resources. Archaeologists call the period after 10,000 B.P. the Archaic period. Because of the variety of cultures that developed based on the use of local plants and animals, the Archaic period is usually identified by region. The Plains Archaic is different from the Desert or Eastern Archaic way of life. Some archaeologists make even narrower distinctions among Southern Plains, Northern Plains, Eastern Plains, and Western Plains. Within each of these geographical groups there are more localized cultures as well.

In western North Dakota, campsites where Archaic people lived for short periods of time have been uncovered. At these sites there have been rare finds of Archaic points made of types of stone that are more common to other geographic areas. The distinctive Knife River flint continues to be an important material for tools. Points made from it have been found far from the area where it occurs naturally, and it seems that people came from long distances to mine the stone. The Archaic people probably made baskets and hide containers like those later used by the Hidatsa and other Indian tribes. The discovery of bone needles suggests that hides were sewn to make clothing, and, possibly, dwellings. There is some evidence that the Indians of the Archaic period lived in tipis, cone-shaped tents made of hides.

Campsites and burial mounds found throughout the United States

The technique of pottery making came to the Plains during the Woodland period, 2,000 to 1,200 years ago. This early 19th-century clay vessel differs little from pots made on the Plains in the Woodland period.

and Canada dated from 2,000 B.P. to 1,200 B.P. contain pottery, stone pipes, shell ornaments, and small stone points. These finds indicate that a major technological and social change had occurred. Archaeologists call this new way of life the Woodland culture because they believe that some aspects of this life-style originated in the forest areas of the eastern United States. Only a few Woodland culture campsites on the Missouri River have been found and excavated. The objects discovered here probably belonged to small groups of buffalo hunters. They wore clothing sewn from animal hides and decorated with shell beads. They fashioned their

PREHISTORIC PEOPLE OF THE GREAT PLAINS

Culture Approx. Date	Events	Climate and Habitat	Fauna	Technology	Subsistence Activities	Social Organization
Paleo-Indian 25,000–14,000 B.P.* 14,000–10,000 B.P.	ancestors of Indians arrive in North America, probably crossing the Bering Strait Paleo-Indians well established throughout North America	Pleistocene—glaciers lower water levels, extend shorelines; forest habitat	large mammals such as mammoth, great bison, ground sloth, saber-toothed tiger, dire wolf, caribou, horse, camel	worked stone projectile points dating to 12,000 B.P. found in Clovis, New Mexico; cultures become more varied	hunting large animals; gathering roots, nuts, fruits, berries	small, seminomadic hunting bands, 15–20 people in group
Archaic Period 10,000–3,000 B.P.		warming—glaciers melt, water level rises, shores recede; deep bays and rivers form; grasslands replace forests; seasonal variation	large animals die out; smaller game animals emerge	barbed or notched points; polished stone choppers and scrapers; grinding stones	hunting bison and small game animals; gathering roots, nuts, fruits, berries	small semipermanent villages; tipi dwellers; seasonal wandering along same route
Plains Woodland Period 2,000–1,200 B.P.	horticulture and pottery making; trade over wide area	seasonal variation	bison, bear, deer, rabbit and other small animals; fish	wide range of tools for horticulture and food preparation; use of bow and arrow; fishing and trapping equipment; pottery and baskets; bone and wood implements; hide clothing, mound burials	hunting bison, bear, deer, and smaller game; fishing and trapping; cultivation of corn, beans, squash; storage of surplus	complex social and religious institutions; trade relationships over wide area
Plains Village 1,000 B.P.–contact with Europeans (16th century)				scaffold burials		permanent villages of earth-covered houses

*Before the present

tools from bone and stone and made engraved pottery. The bow and arrow came into common use during this period. The technique of driving buffalo over cliffs continued as well.

The tipi was the most popular form of housing among the Woodland culture people who lived on the Plains. The Indians sometimes set up large camps on terraces above major waterways. On high bluffs near water but away from the campsites they placed their cemeteries, which were marked by mounds of earth. The dead were usually buried in one mass grave. Each person was buried with his or her own possessions, such as animal-tooth pendants, tools, and shell beads.

Around 900 years ago the people living along the Missouri River began to build log houses covered with earth and practice farming with simple hand

A view of the Missouri River. The Indians built villages on high bluffs overlooking the river. The land nearest the river provided timber for fuel and, when cleared, rich soil for farming.

equipment. Archaeologists do not know whether these people adopted the idea of log houses and horticulture from eastern tribes or whether the farming people moved from the East to the Plains and traveled up the Missouri. The earliest village sites found in the Missouri Valley are south of the area later occupied by the Hidatsa and Mandan. Although archaeological records documenting the movements of people into and out of the region are incomplete, it is evident that this marked the beginning of intensive occupation of the area.

These early villages were built on bluffs overlooking the Missouri River. They were small settlements made up of 20 to 30 rectangular houses. The people grew corn, squash, and beans and hunted buffalo. Bone fishhooks found during excavations at village sites indicate that the inhabitants obtained fish from the river. The pottery and tools of bone and stone found there are very similar to those made and used by later tribes. Because no cemeteries have been found near these villages, archaeologists believe that these people probably placed their dead on scaffolds, or raised platforms. The body was wrapped in buffalo robes, and the remains would eventually be consumed by the elements. This custom was common among the later Plains tribes, including the Hidatsa and Mandan.

This basic village way of life remained stable for many centuries. Although some villages were abandoned and new ones were built, the people continued to live along the Missouri River and its tributaries. Major shifts in village life occurred around 500 years ago, when the shape of the houses changed from rectangular to round and the size of the villages increased. Fortification ditches and walls started to appear around the villages, and large areas for refuse were created. These changes imply improvements in food production and storage, leading to larger village populations. They also point toward a need for protection from hostile outsiders and the probable development of some governing body of leaders to organize these more complex activities. More important, the new way of life is so similar to that of the later Hidatsa and Mandan culture that it marks these tribes' earliest probable presence.

It is difficult to distinguish early Hidatsa villages from those of the Mandan, so the archaeological record has been supplemented by historical evidence to create a clearer picture. Our first real knowledge of the Hidatsa comes from written records made by non-Indian traders and explorers. Many of these early visitors tried to obtain information about the origins of the Hidatsa and the locations of their previous villages. The non-Indians were frustrated, however, when they were told different stories by different people.

The Awatixa, one of the three original groups that would later come together and be known as the Hidatsa tribe, believed that they originated on

Depressions in the surface of the earth, marked by variations in the color of the grass, indicate the long-ago locations of earth lodges. Such depressions are all that remain of the Hidatsa's villages along the Knife River.

the Missouri River when Charred Body, a sacred being, took the form of an arrow and came down from the sky to make a village. Charred Body brought with him 13 couples who became the first Awatixa on earth. He taught the Awatixa everything they needed to know about the world. Through the adventures of Charred Body, First Creator—another sacred being—and the supernatural children (the offspring of the 13 original couples), the tribal hunting rituals known as the *Naxpike*, or Hidebeating Ceremony, and the Buffalo Calling Ceremony originated. The holy founders also put together many

sacred tribal bundles containing objects that held special spiritual powers for the people.

The origin myth of the Awaxawi, another of the three original groups, begins with the creation of the earth by First Creator and Lone Man. These two sacred beings competed with each other to see who could make the best place for people to thrive. On the east side of the Missouri River Lone Man created the open rolling plains, and on the west First Creator made the rugged badlands. While these acts of creation were taking place, the Awaxawi were living inside the earth. Afterward they climbed to the surface on a vine and wandered about until they reached the area that is now central North Dakota. According to legend, the Awaxawi lived for many years in a densely wooded area southeast of the present city of Fargo, North Dakota. During that time some Awaxawi hunters met the Hidatsa at Devils Lake in the northeastern part of North Dakota. The Awaxawi continued to move from place to place for a period of time until they reached the Missouri River, where they met the Awatixa.

The Hidatsa also believed that they had lived within the earth at one time. They had come to the surface near Devils Lake and traveled northward. They wandered around for many years and eventually returned to Devils Lake. A party of their warriors came upon the Missouri River, where they met other people who spoke similar languages and grew corn. The Hidatsa warriors liked the corn, and when they returned to Devils Lake they told the other Hidatsa about it. The people then decided to settle along the Missouri River, too.

The layout of what was once Big Hidatsa village is clearly visible in this aerial view of the excavation site near Stanton, North Dakota.

When they arrived at the Missouri, the Hidatsa encountered the Mandan, who lived at the junction of the Heart and Missouri rivers near what is now the city of Bismarck, North Dakota. The Mandan were afraid of the newcomers and asked them to build their village farther north, but not so far that they would become strangers or enemies. Following the Mandan's request, the Hidatsa settled farther up the Missouri.

A smallpox epidemic in 1781 caused them to resettle along the Knife River, a tributary of the Missouri. A sacred leader of the tribe had promised the people that they would become as numerous as willows when they built their village there. From that time on they called themselves *Hidatsa*—People of the Willows.

Archaeologists have tried to confirm these origin myths by the study of excavations, but only a few places on the Missouri and its tributaries can be accurately identified as Hidatsa, Awatixa, and Awaxawi. Three of these sites are now archaeological excavations known as Big Hidatsa, Sakakawea, and Amahami, respectively. Recent digs at the Flaming Arrow site near Washburn, North Dakota—claimed by the Awatixa to be their ancient home—show that this site was indeed one of the earliest Indian settlements in the area. However, archaeologists could not identify the original inhabitants of the site.

Although the origins of the Hidatsa have not been confirmed by archaeological research, it is clear that they had been following the same way of life for hundreds of years by the time the first Europeans reached the Upper Missouri. Their food, houses, and ceremonies show that they had a thorough understanding of the resources of the area. The Hidatsa and Mandan used the same long-established hunting techniques as the other Plains Indian tribes and, like them, relied on the buffalo for meat, bone, and hides. In addition they grew corn, squash, beans, and sunflowers, which improved their opportunities for survival and provided them with a supply of trade goods. Other tribes in the region regularly visited the Hidatsa's villages to trade for surplus agricultural products. Their favorable reports of the Hidatsa's hospitality and trade goods eventually attracted the first non-Indians to the villages. ▲

A Hidatsa mother and child, photographed by Edward S. Curtis about 1908.

EARLY NON-INDIAN CONTACTS

Long before any Europeans visited the Hidatsa and Mandan villages, some had heard of the two tribes from Assiniboin and Cree Indians who traded with them. As early as the Paleo-Indian period the highly prized Knife River flint had been traded among the people, and a permanent trading network developed from these origins. The Hidatsa and Mandan exchanged surplus corn with other tribes in return for hides and horses. Even the Hidatsa's traditional enemies, such as the Cheyenne, Teton Sioux, and Yanktonai, were guaranteed safety and hospitality when they came to trade. Members of these tribes knew that the Hidatsa rule of conduct said no outsider could be harmed while inside the village: All were to be treated with courtesy and hospitality. The combination of desirable trade goods and a guaranteed welcome attracted traders. As a result of their position in the trade network the Hidatsa and Mandan became wealthy.

As early as 1729 word of the people who lived in permanent villages of earthen huts reached the French-Canadian merchant-trader Pierre Gaultier de Varennes, the Sieur de La Vérendrye, at his post north of Lake Superior. It was not until November 1738, however, that La Vérendrye and his sons, with the aid of a Cree Indian who served as their guide and interpreter, followed the old Mandan trail through what is now northern North Dakota to the Indian villages. His report of the expedition is the earliest known written description of the Mandan.

There is no doubt that La Vérendrye reached the Mandan, but it is impossible to determine the locations of their villages from his description, which does not match any of the village sites known to us today. In addition, the mapping instruments he used to calculate his position were unreliable. Archaeologists believe La Vérendrye visited the Mandan settlements along the Heart River. Because it was the start of winter, the explorers may have been taken to one of the winter villages, which were built on the bottomlands close to the river to protect the people from the chilling wind. The strong fortifications and large number of lodges La Vérendrye encountered, however, suggest that he was received at one of their summer, or permanent, villages. These were built on high terraces farther away from the water so that the houses were not washed away by the annual flooding of the river. La Vérendrye's description of the lodges, pottery, basketry, clothing, and other details matches later reports of the typical Mandan and Hidatsa way of life in their

The Hidatsa cooked much of their food in round-bottomed pots that were placed in the fire's ashes. A separate basketlike ring steadied the pot when it was not in the ashes.

summer villages. In keeping with the Indians' tradition of hospitality, La Vérendrye and his men were well treated by the Mandan, who invited them to many feasts, more than they could possibly attend.

Other explorers after La Vérendrye followed the Mandan trail to the Indian villages. Although these people left few records, it is known from the journals of later visitors that they were independent traders who were not connected with any of the major fur companies that employed trappers and traders to acquire pelts for them. As early as 1776 free traders had taken up residence with the Indians. They married Indian women, learned the native languages, adopted Indian dress, and generally lived like Indians. Some of these resident traders would later become interpreters for the various expeditions that would visit the villages.

In November 1797 the noted Canadian geographer and explorer David Thompson traveled from his trading post on the Assiniboine River to the Indian villages. Thompson, who had traded for the Hudson's Bay Company for several years, was experienced at living on the Plains. His guides were non-Indians who had lived in the villages for a number of years. But temperatures below -30 degrees Fahrenheit and deep snowdrifts delayed his expedition. The journey, which normally took 10 days, took more than a month.

In his journal Thompson referred to the Hidatsa and Mandan as the Willow and the Flying Fall Indians, probably a

After the smallpox epidemic of 1781, the Hidatsa settled along the Knife River, where, as one sacred leader predicted, their descendants would become as numerous as the willows that lined its banks.

partial English translation of their names for themselves. At the time he visited them the Hidatsa were living in three villages along the Knife River, and the Mandan occupied two villages on the Missouri. Thompson estimated the population of the Hidatsa villages to be 1,330 and that of the Mandan to be 1,520. He was curious about the life of the villagers and attempted to learn about their traditions and customs. He wrote that the Indians lived in earthen lodges built to protect them from unfriendly tribes. The interiors of the lodges were furnished with wooden beds raised off the ground that were covered with buffalo hides for warmth and comfort and were surrounded by hide curtains. The Indians cooked their food in pottery jars. The meat of various animals—buffalo, antelope, deer, and bear—was boiled in liquid like a stew rather than roasted over a fire. Often elderly men of the tribe would join a family for the evening meal. Because there were only enough eating utensils for each member of the family, the guests would bring their own, usually wooden or pottery bowls and spoons made of buffalo horn. Thompson also noted the cleanliness of the lodges, the quiet order of the villages, and the hospitality of the villagers.

Late in the fall of 1804 a group of explorers led by Captains Meriwether Lewis and William Clark arrived at the Mandan villages. President Thomas Jefferson had commissioned the expedition to explore the territory stretching from the Missouri River to the Pacific Ocean. Lewis and Clark's journey would produce the first thorough report of the northwestern United States.

Lewis and Clark built a winter camp near the Mandan and spent more than five months among the Indians. Their diaries provide vivid descriptions of Indian life. The two explorers got to know the Mandan and Hidatsa leaders quite well, especially one Hidatsa chief, Le Borgne, who is mentioned by many other visitors as well. Le Borgne, also

This engraving of Meriwether Lewis and William Clark holding council with the Indians appeared in Journal of the Voyages and Travels of a Corps of Discovery under the Command of Captain Lewis and Captain Clark of the Army of the United States, 1804–1806. *The author, Patrick Gass, was a member of the famous expedition.*

known as Kokookis or The One-Eyed, had a reputation as an outstanding warrior, diplomat, and orator. Blind in one eye, he stood six feet tall and was well muscled. When Lewis and Clark met the Hidatsa chief, he was about 45 years old and at the height of his power. Because of Le Borgne's size and personality Clark considered him the most powerful Hidatsa leader of the time. In recognition of his importance, Lewis gave him a flag, a shirt, medals, armbands, scarlet cloth, and other gifts.

Although some non-Indians thought that Le Borgne's actions were at times cruel and arrogant, many found him hospitable and helpful. When a fur trader with the Northwest Company, one of the fur companies that employed trappers and traders in the area, wanted to begin trading with the Crow tribe, Le Borgne arranged for a Crow Indian he had adopted as a brother in a ceremony of friendship to guide and protect the expedition party. The Hidatsa chief sent the party off with a two-hour speech. Le Borgne also helped to arrange a meeting between the Cheyenne Indians and another Northwest Company trader. He was protective of Indians in distress as well. Once when visiting the Cheyenne, Le

Borgne had prevented them from killing several Assiniboin Indians by walking around the captives, brandishing his battle ax, and threatening to kill the first man to harm an Assiniboin.

Among other Hidatsa leaders mentioned by Lewis and Clark were Wolf Chief, White Wolf, and Black Moccasin. Like Le Borgne, these men had reputations for bravery and treated the explorers well. Black Moccasin, the chief of Awatixa village, often spent evenings with Lewis and Clark, telling them the history of his people. Years later, in 1832, when the artist George Catlin visited the tribe, Black Moccasin inquired about Long Knife and Red Hair, as Lewis and Clark were called by the Hidatsa, and wished he could see them again.

These early contacts between Indians and non-Indians served as important examples for future explorers and traders. Because the first non-Indians were well received, traders were attracted to the Knife River villages, and the area became a commercial center for the Upper Missouri. The hospitality shown by the Hidatsa and Mandan encouraged non-Indians to stop at the Indian settlements for trade goods, supplies, and assistance. In later years the two tribes would boast of their constant support for American and Canadian explorers and traders and would point out that they had never made war on any non-Indians.

Within a few years of Lewis and Clark's expedition, large parties of traders and people curious about the Indi-

(continued on page 36)

A reproduction of the medal given by Lewis and Clark to Indian leaders they encountered during their exploration of the northwestern United States. Although this medal was minted more recently, such medals were issued by the U.S. government in 1904 to celebrate the 100th anniversary of the expedition.

THE LEWIS AND CLARK EXPEDITION

In 1804, Captains Meriwether Lewis and William Clark set out to explore the western territory recently acquired by the United States from France in the Louisiana Purchase. On May 14, the explorers left St. Louis. They sailed up the Missouri River and reached the Mandan village of Mih-tutta-hang-kush in the fall. The Mandan were known to be friendly, so Lewis and Clark decided to build a camp nearby in order to get corn and information about the western terrain. While there they hired Toussaint Charbonneau, a French trader and trapper living in the Hidatsa village of Awatixa, to be a guide and interpreter. When the party left the Indian settlement the following spring, Charbonneau's Indian wife, Sacajawea, and their infant son went with them as well.

Charbonneau had settled in Awatixa almost 10 years earlier. He knew several Indian languages and had some knowledge of the geography of the western United States, gained in his travels as a trapper. His young wife, the only woman among more than 30 men on the expedition, would make important contributions to its success. Sacajawea had been born about 1788 into the Shoshone tribe. As a young girl she had been captured by the Hidatsa, who named her Tsakakawias, or Bird Woman, and sold her to Charbonneau.

Sacajawea was in her late teens when she accompanied her husband and the explorers, who sought a route to the Pacific Ocean. Only a few months earlier she had given birth to a son, Jean-Baptiste. Throughout the expedition the presence of Sacajawea and her baby would signal all Indians encountered along the way that the explorers meant no harm. Her courage and cheerfulness quickly won her the admiration and affection of Lewis and Clark. Shortly after the party set out in the spring of 1805, the explorers' maps, compasses, food, and medicine were tossed out of the canoe in which Sacajawea was riding when a storm blew up unexpectedly. The quick-

Meriwether Lewis, the leader of the expedition sent by President Thomas Jefferson to explore the northwestern United States.

A statue of Sacajawea in Bismarck, North Dakota.

thinking Sacajawea, her baby balanced across her lap, leaned dangerously over the side of the canoe and retrieved the goods.

Sacajawea's ability to speak the Shoshone language as well as her knowledge of local plant foods, medicinal herbs, and the western terrain were invaluable to the explorers. She recognized landmarks of the Rocky Mountain territory from her childhood, including the place where she had been captured. When food supplies were low, she gathered berries and goose eggs from the surroundings, dug up wild artichokes buried by prairie dogs, and made broth from elk bones.

When the party finally met up with the Shoshone, Captain Lewis tried to convince the chief to give them some horses and men to serve as guides. The Indians were suffering from lack of food and were not about to interrupt a hunting trip. Clark, unable to make himself understood by the Shoshone chief, sent for Sacajawea. Keeping her head down as she approached the chief, she prepared to translate his words to the explorers. At his first words she realized, to her surprise, that he was her brother, Cameahwait. After a warm reunion she persuaded him to grant the explorer's wishes.

The expedition reached the Pacific Ocean in November 1805. They spent the winter along the coast and on March 23, 1806, began their return trip to St. Louis. Once back at the Mandan village, Charbonneau, Sacajawea, and their son left the party. Charbonneau was paid $500.33 for his services, but Sacajawea received no fee for hers. The courageous Indian woman, of whom Clark wrote, "She has been of great service to me as a pilot through this country," has inspired statues and monuments throughout the region she helped explore.

An 1838 engraving of an Ohio River steamboat. With improved methods of water travel, the Hidatsa and Mandan villages became popular stopping places for scientists, artists, and adventure seekers.

(continued from page 33)

ans sailed up the Missouri on riverboats from St. Louis. Among the passengers to make the trip were the scientists Henry Marie Brackenridge and John Bradbury, who left good accounts of the native plants and animals as well as of the people.

In the 1830s, when steamboats began making regular trips up the Missouri River, others interested in the Indians began visiting the Hidatsa and Mandan. Two of them were George Catlin and the German scholar Maximilian Alexander Philippe, prince of Wied Neuwied. Both wrote lengthy, illustrated descriptions that are important sources of information about life in the villages at that time. Like Lewis and Clark, these later visitors took the opportunity to get to know the Indians as

friends and tried to learn about their way of life.

Catlin spent a few weeks in the summer of 1832 at the Mandan and Hidatsa villages. Through his portraits and scenes of Indian life Catlin hoped to depict Indians as they really were. As a boy, he had been intrigued by stories of the frontier and often hunted for Indian relics in the woods near his Pennsylvania home. Although he practiced law for several years, he preferred to earn his living as a painter. When Catlin saw a group of Indians passing through Philadelphia, his dream of portraying Indians was born. Neither Catlin's friends nor his family supported his idea, but he was determined to pursue his dream. In the summer of 1832 he boarded the steamboat *The Yellowstone* for a trip up the Missouri River to Fort Union, a trading post at the mouth of the Yellowstone River. After painting there for several weeks, Catlin joined two French traders who were traveling by canoe down the Missouri to St. Louis. After about a week, they arrived at the Mandan villages.

Although Catlin stayed primarily at the Mandan village of Mitutanka, he visited the Hidatsa villages. Catlin estimated the total population of the Hidatsa to be 1,500 people. He thought the Hidatsa's biggest village was made up of 40 to 50 earth lodges. At Awatixa he spent a few days in the home of the old chief, Black Moccasin. During his stay there, a party of Crow Indians arrived. Catlin painted portraits of them as well as of Black Moccasin, Two Crows, Two Crows's wife, and several other Hidatsa men and women. He crossed the Knife River in a bullboat, a round-bottomed craft made from willows and hides, participated in a horse race (a favorite sport of the Hidatsa), and went on a buffalo hunt.

Catlin's paintings and letters are an important record of summer life in the Mandan and Hidatsa villages, but the reports of Prince Maximilian, who spent a winter among the two tribes, provide greater detail. He was accompanied by his servant, David Dreidoppel, and the artist Karl Bodmer. The party arrived at Fort Clark, several miles below the Knife River villages, on June 18, 1833. Their steamboat, the *Assiniboin*, was met by a large crowd of Indians, including the popular Mandan

The Hidatsa's bullboats, which carried people and goods across the river, were made of willow branches and covered with hides.

chief, Four Bears, and Two Crows, the Hidatsa leader painted by Catlin the previous summer. The independent trader Toussaint Charbonneau was also in the group and served as interpreter for the Hidatsa leaders who met the boat.

Prince Maximilian, Bodmer, and Dreidoppel did not disembark at Fort Clark but remained on the boat all the way to Fort Union, then boarded a smaller boat and sailed upriver to Fort McKenzie, where they stayed about a month. In mid-September they left Fort McKenzie and on November 8, 1833, arrived back at Fort Clark, where they planned to spend the winter.

Wintering at Fort Clark provided Maximilian and Bodmer with plenty of time to experience Mandan and Hidatsa culture. They spent the first few days at Fort Clark getting settled into their quarters. On November 13, Maximilian recorded in his journal that Four Bears had brought his wife and son to visit. The Mandan chief would continue to visit him regularly throughout the winter. Yellow Feather was another Mandan who became a close friend of the explorers.

On November 26, Maximilian, Bodmer, and Charbonneau were invited to witness a Hidatsa medicine ceremony. Known as Walking with the Daughters-in-law or the Painted Red Stick, the ceremony was held to bring the buffalo close to the village so the men

Balls constructed of animal hide and sewn with sinew were used in a variety of games.

would not have to go far to hunt. During the first part of the ceremony, six men dressed in their finest clothes and carrying sticks decorated with buffalo-hoof rattles sang and imitated the sounds of buffalo. Following the singing there was a feast during which they asked the spirits for success in hunting and warfare. After that there was more singing and dancing.

The next day the visitors toured the Hidatsa's winter village and watched the Indians play winter games. They saw young men throwing spears at a leather hoop that they rolled along the ground. The man who could direct his spear through the hoop to stop it from rolling won. The visitors watched as women bounced leather balls on their feet, the winner being the person who bounced the ball the most times. Children played ice games on the frozen river.

On their second day at the Hidatsa village Maximilian and his party visited the lodge of Yellow Bear and attended a dance held by the women to pray for good crops for the coming year. The Hidatsa believed that there was a spirit living deep within every person and that these spirits could be brought out during ceremonies. For instance, a corn spirit resided in the stomach of the head dancer of the group. Maximilian reported that during the ceremony the head dancer went into a trance and an ear of corn appeared in her mouth. One of the other dancers then pushed the ear back down the woman's throat.

Karl Bodmer, the Swiss artist whose paintings are regarded as accurate representations of Plains Indian life in the 1830s.

After three days the party returned to Fort Clark, where they found that most of the Mandan had left for their winter villages. Although these villages were farther away from the fort than their summer villages were, the Mandan continued to travel to the post to talk with the visitors and trade for food and ammunition. Maximilian spent many long hours in conversation with Four Bears and the Hidatsa leader The Road-Maker. He also visited the Mandan villages and attended ceremonies. Sometimes the dancers held their ceremonies at the fort: In February a group of Hidatsa came to hold a scalp dance to celebrate a successful attack on an enemy.

Maximilian recorded all his conversations and observations in small leather-covered notebooks. After his return to Germany he used his notes to write a book about his experiences. Karl Bodmer's sketches and paintings of the Mandan and Hidatsa people, their ceremonies, and the surrounding scenery accompanied Maximilian's writings. Bodmer's goal was to produce a visual record that would substantiate and illustrate what Maximilian had written in his journal. Together the paintings and writings provide a detailed picture of life in the Mandan and Hidatsa villages.

Catlin and Prince Maximilian visited the villages just before a smallpox epidemic nearly destroyed the Indians they had documented and befriended. Their accounts provide important information about a way of life that would soon be disrupted. ▲

Good Bear and his family, photographed by Edward S. Curtis about 1908.

LIFE
IN THE
KNIFE RIVER
VILLAGES

The non-Indians who encountered the Hidatsa and Mandan brought not only useful items such as horses, guns, and metal utensils, but also diseases to which the Indians had no immunity. Smallpox, measles, and whooping cough were deadly to the Indians. Earlier epidemics had raged through the Hidatsa villages, but the outbreak of smallpox in 1837 was by far the most disastrous and devastating to afflict the two tribes. Sixty to 70 percent of the Hidatsa and Mandan population died. Many families were left without men to hunt for them, and there were not enough warriors to protect the village from hostile tribes. Even worse than the decline of the villages, however, was the death of men who owned sacred bundles. Only certain people could perform the ceremonies associated with the sacred bundles, and the rights and knowledge to perform these ceremonies had to be passed on by the men

who held the bags. When these men died suddenly without teaching the rituals to someone else, the bundles became useless.

The smallpox epidemic of 1837 caused physical death and psychological trauma. Knowledge and skills disappeared almost overnight. By 1839 the Hidatsa and Mandan cultures that George Catlin and Prince Maximilian had described in such detail had all but perished. Although that life had never been easy, the Plains Indians had developed ways of coping with the difficulties caused by unpredictable weather and migratory animal populations. Temperatures could range from 30 degrees below zero to more than 100 degrees above. Constant strong winds endangered the lives of hunters in winter and dried out the gardens and grasslands in summer. The rains that were necessary for the crops sometimes caused floods or came at the wrong

A herd of buffalo grazes on the Plains.

time; sometimes they did not come at all. The buffalo herds were usually dependable, but when water was scarce and grass parched, the herds might not follow their usual migration routes. The oral histories of all the Plains tribes are filled with stories of starvation, freezing, and drowning.

Their Missouri Valley location made life a little more predictable for the Hidatsa and Mandan than for some of the other Plains Indians. The river created a wide floodplain that formed two or three levels of terraced land. The terrace nearest the river was densely wooded. The Indians felled the trees, leaving rich soil that was ideal for farming. Every year the spring floods replenished the soil but washed away anything near the river. For this reason the Indians built their permanent villages on the higher terraces farther back from the river. These treeless terraces were cooled by the wind in summer, but that same wind made them frigid in the winter. The Hidatsa sought the woods and protection of the lower floodplain for their winter villages.

Summer was the busiest time of year. It was a time of hard work both in the fields and on the hunt, a time when the major ceremonies and dances were held. But it was also a time for swimming, horse and foot racing, ball games, and gambling.

A Hidatsa summer village generally contained 80 to 100 earth-covered houses. It was built on a grassy plain above the Knife River and stretched toward the gently rolling hills. The lodges were not arranged in any particular order and their tunnellike entryways faced in all directions. As a result, visitors could easily get lost. Racks for drying food, dog houses, hide tanning frames, and other structures that filled the open spaces between the lodges added to the confusion. A sturdy log stockade with two openings for access surrounded the village. Outside the stockade were fields of corn and pastures for horses. Each field was care-fully planned and fenced to keep out the horses. Between the fields and the pastures was a level place for the children to play. Away from the village, up on a hill, stood burial scaffolds and memorial shrines, arrangements of rocks or bones placed in the cemetery by the relatives of the dead.

The Hidatsa built two kinds of earth lodges. One style had a flat roof, and the other had a domed roof. Both styles were constructed the same way. Four large, upright posts about 10 feet long were placed in the center of the lodge. These logs formed a square and, when the lodge was complete, would serve as the location for the fireplace. At the tops of these vertical posts the Hidatsa placed four horizontal beams. The walls of the lodge were made of shorter logs

A typical domed-roof earth lodge with some of the roof covering removed to show its construction. In the foreground is a rack used for drying vegetables, meat, and roots.

set upright in the earth several feet away from the central posts. These logs were placed close together in a circle, and an opening was left for the door. The roof was made by laying small logs from the walls to the horizontal beams in the center. Because the central beams were higher than the walls, the roof sloped, creating a domed dwelling. In building the flat-roofed lodges the hole for the fireplace was partially filled in with logs trimmed to the exact length of the opening. This required more work, but the Indians preferred the flat roof to the domed because people could sit on it. When the main supports, walls, and roof had been built, willow branches were laid over them. Then everything was covered with grass matting. After this, the roof and walls were covered with sod blocks—bricklike chunks of root-matted earth—or with loose earth. If the Indians used sod blocks, they cut the earth with hoes, then carried the blocks to the roof and pounded each one firmly in place. Loose earth was dumped onto the roof, where it was smoothed and packed to make a solid cover. Because heavy rains could wash away the loose earth, sod roofs were considered better. A typical Hidatsa earth lodge measured 40 feet in diameter and could hold 40 to 50 people. Some lodges used for ceremonies were larger and held as many as 200 people.

The interiors of the earth lodges varied from family to family, but there were general similarities. Just inside the door were corrals for the best horses, those the Indians valued most. A wall of posts served as a windbreak between the entryway and the living area. It also provided privacy for the family and security from dogs and other animals not allowed beyond the partition.

The fireplace, a shallow pit built within the four center support posts, was the heart of the household. The women lined the pit with rocks to contain the fire and spread willow mats and buffalo robes around it for people to sit upon while lounging or working. A sick child or elder might sleep next to the fire. Above the fireplace, cooking pots and wet moccasins hung from a horizontal pole that extended diagonally from one support post to another.

Along the wall were beds and storage platforms. The beds, wooden platforms covered with buffalo hides, were partitioned off with hide curtains for privacy. A woman kept her workbag containing needles and other tools used for sewing, as well as the material for the project she was working on, under her bed. The Indians stored clothing, pottery, food, and other objects on beds that were not being used and built smaller platforms between the beds for additional storage. Some clothing and food were kept out of the way in hide bags that hung from the lodge's rafters. The Indians also stored food in pits dug into the floor of the lodge. These pits held dried corn, squash, and beans, as well as dried meat and other foods that would be used when the family re-

The interior of a Mandan earth lodge, painted by Karl Bodmer. The Indians kept their best horses inside the lodge to protect them from the elements and from being stolen by other Indians.

turned to the summer house the following spring. Some pits were so deep that the Indians needed a log ladder to climb down into them. Empty pits that were dirty or whose walls were caving in were filled with garbage and then covered over permanently.

Between the fireplace and one wall was a sacred area where ceremonial objects were kept and some rituals were performed. Sometimes the area was curtained off to conceal it from strangers. Even when it was open, however, no one was allowed to walk through the area or play in it. In order to get from one side of the earth lodge to the other, the people had to walk around the fireplace to avoid the sacred area.

Most Plains Indians built sweat lodges, structures used for purification and prayer, outside their houses. Some Hidatsa dwellings, however, were large enough to contain a sweat lodge inside.

Long Soldier and his two wives,
photographed in the late 19th century.
Many Hidatsa men had several wives, who
were usually sisters or cousins.

The bentwood frame of the sweat lodge was placed in a corner near the door of the house. When in use, the frame was covered with hides or blankets. Heated stones were then placed inside and sprinkled with water to produce steam. The steam carried the Indians' prayers to the various spirits that guided their lives.

The earth lodges were built by women. Because each earth lodge was considered sacred, as the central support beams were put in place the builders petitioned the spirits to protect the house and fill it with happiness. Each house was owned by a group of women who were closely related. Hidatsa society was matrilocal: When a woman married, she and her husband usually came to live with her family in her mother's lodge.

The Hidatsa were organized into large family groups known as clans. Clans took care of their own members and looked after widows and orphans who had no adult men to provide for them. Clans also disciplined their members, especially young boys, when they were too mischievous. Children belonged to their mother's clan and were members of that clan all their life. Everyone in the same clan was related. There were members of every clan in all three Hidatsa communities, so every person had relatives in each village. No one could marry a member of his or her own clan but instead had to choose a spouse who was a member of another clan. This meant that every person had ties to his or her mother's clan, his or her father's clan, and the clan of the person he or she married.

Among the Hidatsa some men practiced polygyny, or marriage to more than one woman. A good hunter in particular might have more than one wife because of the added food—and hence added work—he brought in. A man had to support all his wives equally well and keep them happy. Because all the wives lived in the same lodge, a man usually married sisters, who were members of the same clan.

The Hidatsa followed a kinship system that grouped people together based on age and sex. People of the same age and sex as a child's grandmother were called grandmother. People of the same age and sex as a child's grandfather were called grandfather. Children called their mother's sisters and all their father's wives "mother." This made sense to the Hidatsa because a man could have more than one wife and these wives were usually sisters. Children called their father's brothers "father" because they were the same age and sex as their father. The father's sister and her husband and the mother's brother and his wife were called aunt and uncle. The Hidatsa did not distinguish between stepbrothers and stepsisters or half brothers and half sisters; because all of a man's wives were usually sisters and members of the same clan, all of their children were brothers and sisters and members of the same clan. Other relatives were also considered brothers, sisters, grandmothers, and grandfathers, so that a Hidatsa child would have many close relatives to look after him or her.

Each village had a council of elders who were selected from among the heads of families in the community. The council made decisions regarding the welfare of the village, such as when to hold a buffalo hunt and whether the people should go to war. When an elder left the council or died, the other council members selected a replacement, usually a person who as a younger man had proven himself an outstanding warrior and hunter.

Hidatsa men and women belonged to societies that carried out different social and religious functions within the village. The men's societies were involved mainly in hunting and warfare: Some guarded the people against enemy warriors during the hunt; others had duties associated with tribal ceremonies. The women's societies were related to farming, buffalo hunting, and celebrating men's war victories. Membership in a society was a sign of social status, and some societies were ranked higher than others. A person who wanted to join a particular society gave gifts of hides or other goods to the members to demonstrate his or her desire to be admitted to the group. All the members would then decide whether the person should be allowed to join. Only those with exceptional skills or accomplishments were admitted into the top-ranking societies.

The fields, pastures, and cemetery were located outside the village. Like the earth lodges, the fields were owned by the women. They were placed in the bottomlands near the river, where the ground was fertile and easy to work. Before traders introduced hoes with iron blades, the women used hoes made from the shoulder blades of buffalo and wooden digging-sticks for turning the soil.

Hidatsa women were skillful horticulturalists who planted various crops in the same field to achieve the best results. First they planted several different varieties of sunflowers in mid-spring. When the wild gooseberry bushes came into leaf in late May or early June they planted corn. They placed six to eight kernels in separate hills of dirt that were set well apart. Between each corn hill, the women planted beans, and between every 8 to 10 rows of corn they planted a row of squash.

The Hidatsa grew nine varieties of corn. Because the different varieties mixed easily, forming a cross between two types of corn, each variety was planted in a separate garden. Each type was used for different purposes. Hard white corn was pounded and boiled in water to make a mush of cornmeal. Soft white corn was dried, ground, and mixed with animal fat to make cornballs. Some types of corn were roasted or boiled.

The women planted squash in early June. They sprouted the seeds before sowing them. Once harvested, slices of small squashes were placed on drying racks and dried in the sun for use in the winter.

Immediately after the squash was planted the women planted beans. The Hidatsa grew five varieties of beans. Each type had a different name and was planted, harvested, and stored separately.

The fields were considered sacred. To keep the crops safe from pestilence and destruction, one of the women's societies prayed to the corn spirits to watch over them. All women spent time in the gardens, singing corn songs to facilitate growth, hoeing, and scaring away birds. Women were not supposed to argue near the fields because harsh words could scare away the corn spirits and destroy the crop.

Men and boys attended to the horses, hunted, and protected the village. Young boys hunted birds, collected eggs, and set snares for rabbits. Often they made games out of these pursuits and in the process learned to be good hunters. The food they provided was used by the family, which reinforced the boys' pride in their accomplishments.

Teenage boys were in charge of pasturing and watering the horses. While they watched the horses, boys practiced riding, roping, archery, and throwing games that helped improve the skills they would later need for hunting and warfare. In the late afternoon they drove the horses to the river to water them and went for a swim. Anyone working or playing outside the village was in danger from enemy warriors, so the boys also acted as watches or guards. Caring for horses and guarding the village required responsible individuals, and those young men who performed these duties well were identified as potential village leaders of the future.

Adult men spent most of their time hunting. The Hidatsa preferred the buffalo over all other game because of the

(continued on page 57)

PAINTING THE HIDATSA AND THE MANDAN

Two artists, George Catlin and Karl Bodmer, visited the Hidatsa and Mandan villages early in the 19th century. Their paintings show Plains Indian life before it all but perished under pressures from non-Indian settlers.

Catlin, a self-taught artist, left Philadelphia to become a graphic historian of the American Indians. In 1832 he spent several weeks among the Mandan and Hidatsa, painting and writing about them. For the next five years he traveled throughout the United States, documenting Indian life with his pen and paintbrush. In 1837 he exhibited more than 450 paintings in New York, Washington, Boston, and Philadelphia. His book, Letters and Notes on the Manners, Customs, and Conditions of North American Indians, *which was illustrated with his artwork, was published in London in 1841.*

Catlin Painting the Portrait of Mah-to-toh-pa—Mandan (Four Bears) *by George Catlin, 1857–69.*

Bodmer, a young Swiss artist, accompanied the German scholar Maximilian, prince of Wied-Neuwied, on an expedition along the Missouri River. They spent the winter of 1833–34 at Fort Clark, near the Mandan.

In 1837, only a few years after Catlin's and Bodmer's visits, the Mandan and Hidatsa cultures were almost totally destroyed by a smallpox epidemic. But these artists' works survive, providing accurate and vivid views into the world of the people of the Plains.

Buffalo Chase—Single Death *by George Catlin, 1832–33.*

Black Moccasin, Aged Chief *by George Catlin, 1832.*

**Bull Dance,
Mandan O-Kee-Pa
Ceremony** *by
George Catlin, 1832.*

Bison-Dance of the Mandan Indians, *aquatint engraving after a painting by Karl Bodmer.*

Péhriska-Rúhpa (Two
Ravens), Hidatsa Man,
*watercolor and pencil
by Karl Bodmer, 1834.*

Mid-day Sun, A Pretty Girl *by George Catlin, 1832.*

Hidatsa Village, Earth-Covered Lodges, on Knife River, 1,180 Miles Above St. Louis *by George Catlin, 1832.*

Mató-Tópe (Four Bears), Mandan Chief *by Karl Bodmer.*

Mih-Tutta-Hangkusch, A Mandan Village, *aquatint engraving after a painting by Karl Bodmer.*

(continued from page 48)

greater amount of meat and the useful hides. However, the Indians also hunted deer, antelope, elk, and grizzly bear as well as such smaller animals as beaver, rabbit, and raccoon. Hunting was hard and dangerous work and a constant necessity. The meat the men brought back to the village was shared with those who were unable to hunt. The family of a hardworking hunter ate and dressed better than the family of a lazy hunter.

After the fields were planted, most of the people left the village to hunt buffalo. They set up a temporary camp about 100 to 200 miles away from their permanent village. They built conical tipis out of hide stretched over a foundation of tall poles.

Although individuals and small groups hunted buffalo throughout the year, the large summer hunts were highly organized. One man was chosen by the council of elders to direct the hunt. He was selected on the basis of his own hunting skills and his ability to keep the people working well together. The hunt leader was aided by the Black Mouth men's society that policed the area looking for enemy warriors.

After the camp was established and the herd located, the leader planned the strategy to be used in the hunt. A successful hunt required the cooperation of all the men and the help of the buffalo themselves. The keepers of the sacred bundles used specifically in ceremonies related to the buffalo petitioned the animals to permit themselves to be killed. They promised the buffalo a great feast in their honor at a later date. They also made an offering to the buffalo, frequently of tobacco smoke, asking them not to injure any of the hunters.

At a signal from the hunt leader, the men rode specially trained horses used only for hunting buffalo into the middle of the herd and killed as many animals as they needed. This was a dangerous undertaking because a buffalo could hook a horse with its horns or the horse could stumble, causing the hunter to be thrown under the hooves of the stampeding herd. A surefooted horse that could sense what the buffalo were going to do was so highly valued that it was not used at other times for fear it would be injured, and the time the man had spent in training it would be wasted. These special buffalo horses were kept inside the earth lodges and were rarely sold or given away.

When enough buffalo were killed, the men butchered the animals and brought the meat back to camp for the women to preserve. Each woman took as much meat as was needed for her family, sliced it into pieces, and placed it on racks to dry in the sun. Everyone got some meat, but large households that had several women usually received more because each woman in the family would contribute to the household's reserve. When a family's needs were met, a woman might help another woman so that she had enough for her family.

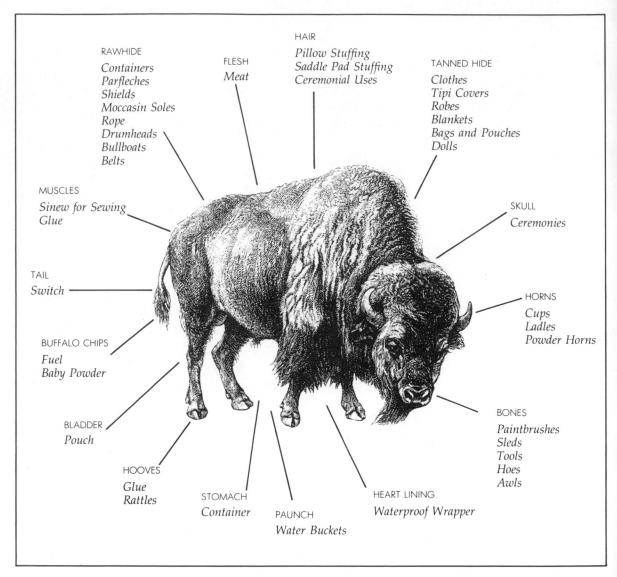

HAIR
Pillow Stuffing
Saddle Pad Stuffing
Ceremonial Uses

RAWHIDE
Containers
Parfleches
Shields
Moccasin Soles
Rope
Drumheads
Bullboats
Belts

FLESH
Meat

TANNED HIDE
Clothes
Tipi Covers
Robes
Blankets
Bags and Pouches
Dolls

MUSCLES
Sinew for Sewing
Glue

SKULL
Ceremonies

TAIL
Switch

HORNS
Cups
Ladles
Powder Horns

BUFFALO CHIPS
Fuel
Baby Powder

BLADDER
Pouch

BONES
Paintbrushes
Sleds
Tools
Hoes
Awls

HOOVES
Glue
Rattles

STOMACH
Container

PAUNCH
Water Buckets

HEART LINING
Waterproof Wrapper

The buffalo was the most important animal the Plains Indians hunted. Practically all of the buffalo—the meat, bones, hide, internal organs, and other body parts—was used in some manner by the Indians.

The men were also responsible for protecting the people against attacks from hostile Indian tribes. Warfare was so common that it was integrated into the social and ceremonial life of the tribe. Boys were expected to grow up to be warriors as well as hunters. A young man participated in war parties and, with the help of a strong spiritual protector, earned a good war record.

Men who were successful in war received public praise in the form of parades, victory dances, and war names. Successful warriors earned the right to decorate themselves and their clothing with symbols of their exploits and added animal tails, feathers, and other symbols to their outfits. Military accomplishments also brought membership in the men's societies that directed village affairs.

The goal of warfare was not to kill, but to demonstrate bravery and skill. Military exploits were judged according to the bravery required; the most honored warriors were those with the most highly valued exploits. Because there was more risk involved in touching a live enemy, the Indians considered this act of higher honor than touching a dead enemy or even killing an enemy in battle. The highest honor a warrior could achieve was for going far from home by himself and killing an enemy in revenge for another's death. Other honors were given to the first four men to touch a dead enemy and to any man who crept into an enemy camp and stole horses.

During the summer men and women made and repaired equipment, tools, utensils, and other articles they would use throughout the year. The Hidatsa's technology was extensive and complex. Women tanned hides; made clothing, pots, and dishes; and wove baskets and reed mats for household use. Men made hunting equipment and sacred objects such as rattles and drums for ceremonial purposes. The Indians used many items that were made out of hide. Rawhide envelopelike bags, called parfleches, were used for storing clothing and sacred items. They used tanned hide for clothing, robes, quivers, shields, drums, and balls, among other objects. Leather was also used for horse gear, bridles, and saddles. From the bones of animals they made farming implements, knives, arrowheads, and sticks used in the various games they played. From stone they fashioned arrowheads, which were used for knives and spear points as well. The Knife River flint found in the nearby quarries continued to be widely used and traded throughout the northern Plains.

The Indians made rakes, bowls, ladles, spoons, grinding mortars and pestles, backrests, and bed frames, as well as other household furnishings, from wood. Branches of willow or ash served as the framework for bullboats, the Hidatsa's typical mode of water travel. The boats were made by the women, who stretched hides over the wooden framework to create a watertight vessel.

Some crafts, such as making baskets and pottery and building houses, could be practiced only by those who owned the right to perform them. For example, only a few people in the tribe possessed the right to make baskets. A person who needed a basket would go to one of these individuals and pay that person hides or other goods to make a basket. People acquired the right to a craft by paying someone who already owned

A Hidatsa basket used for gathering corn. The craft of basket making could be practiced only by those women who owned the right to the skill.

the right to teach his or her knowledge to them. A person could sell the right to a skill to three other people. If the right were sold to a fourth person, the seller lost his or her own right to practice the skill.

The use of sacred bundles in the tribe's major ceremonies was also governed by rights. The owner could sell the right to perform the dances, songs, and prayers that called forth the bundle's supernatural powers three times. With the fourth sale, the owner lost the right to perform the rituals himself. The practice of buying craft and ritual rights helped regulate Hidatsa society. Because it allowed only a few individuals to practice a skill, a small group of experts developed and a certain level of quality was achieved and maintained.

The rights system also placed a value on the ability to perform a skill and insured that people were compensated for their knowledge and expertise.

Personal spiritual quests and many of the tribe's major ceremonies took place during the summer. Among the Hidatsa, relationships with the spiritual world depended on having a personal spiritual protector and a sacred bundle. By enduring hardships, a young man would attract the pity of a spirit who would agree to help him in future endeavors. The young man would spend several days at some distance from the village going without food, drink, or sleep and praying to receive a spiritual protector.

Fasting, prayer, and sleeplessness were important aspects of sacrifice. So was self-mutilation. A Hidatsa man might cut off part of a finger, suspend himself from thongs that pierced his skin, or drag buffalo skulls attached to thongs inserted through his skin in order to attract very powerful spirits. He might have a vision in which the spirit appeared, teaching him sacred songs and instructing him how to prepare his sacred bundles with objects sacred to the spirit. Having a powerful spiritual protector meant that the man would be a successful hunter and warrior.

Although an individual's spiritual quest resulted in a personal sacred bundle with special meaning only to himself, most men also had sacred tribal and clan bundles that were used in the tribe's major ceremonies. These bundles were inherited from the holy people who founded the tribe and represented the origins of the Hidatsa way of life. There were two basic groups of tribal ceremonies: those associated with agriculture and those associated with buffalo hunting. The first agricultural ceremony of the year, known as the Old Woman Who Never Dies Ceremony, was held in the spring, when the water birds returned from the south. The water birds brought the corn spirits with them, and the ceremony was held to make the crops grow well. Other ceremonies were held throughout the summer to bring rain for the fields, scare away insects, and provide general protection for the crops. The last agricultural ceremony of the year was held in the fall, when the water birds took the corn spirits south for the winter.

The hunting ceremonies ranged from individual rituals to major tribal ceremonies that lasted several days. The Naxpike ceremony and the Buffalo Calling Ceremony were the most important hunting ceremonies. The Naxpike, or Hidebeating Ceremony (also called the Sun Dance), was performed to obtain the supernatural hunting and warfare powers contained in a sacred tribal or clan bundle. The powers in these bundles were often passed from generation to generation within a family: A young warrior frequently participated in the Naxpike to obtain the transfer of power from his father's (or anyone he called father) sacred bundle. Men who had demonstrated bravery and wisdom would ask permission of the elders to participate in the cere-

Members of the White Buffalo Cow Society, the most prestigious women's society in Mandan culture, perform a dance to bring the buffalo closer to the village. This engraving, from a painting by Karl Bodmer, was done about 1840.

mony. It involved four days of fasting, dancing, and self-mutilation, and only those with good records received permission to pledge the ceremony. Other men also participated, but they did not have the same amount of responsibility as the pledger. They fasted and danced to receive messages from their spiritual protectors.

The Buffalo Calling Ceremony was held during the winter to bring the buffalo close to the village so the men would not have to go far to hunt in the cold weather. The ceremony required

absolute silence; all wood chopping and other noisy work had to be done beforehand. Even the dogs were muzzled to keep them from barking.

In mid-October, the people began to prepare for the move to the winter villages. These smaller villages were located near the water, where there was plenty of wood. Often the villagers returned to a site they had used before. If the lodges from the previous winter were still standing and suitable for use, the people would just move back in. If, however, the spring floods had dam-

A sketch of the village of Awatixa, which was deserted by the Indians after the smallpox epidemic of 1837. The map, drawn by Sitting Rabbit, appeared in volume I of Collections of the State Historical Society of North Dakota, *published in 1906.*

aged them, new ones would need to be built. Because people expected the winter lodges to be washed away in the spring, they put less effort into building the dwellings.

Except during the times when the people observed the Buffalo Calling Ceremony, life in the winter village was quiet and relaxed. If the summer hunt and the crops had been good, there was plenty of food. Wood and water were nearby. Everyone enjoyed playing winter games, and storytelling helped to pass the long evenings in the lodge.

Adapting their lives to the seasons helped the Hidatsa cope with the rigorous conditions of the northern Plains. They were usually able to deal with the hazards of the environment, but they faced a more formidable human enemy—the Sioux. Sioux was the name the non-Indians gave to seven allied, but dissimilar, tribes. Some of these tribes were tipi-using nomads, whereas others were horticulturalists, and still others forest dwellers. The nomadic tribes supplemented their diet with corn acquired in trade from the Hidatsa and Mandan. As long as the Sioux could get the produce they needed at what they thought was a fair trade, relations were friendly. However, if the Sioux did not have the hides to trade or if there was no surplus corn, they might use force to acquire the food. Eventually, the Sioux and the Hidatsa were engaged in almost continual strife, each side trying to get revenge for past injuries, and the original reasons for the warfare were forgotten. The stockades around the Hidatsa villages usually protected the people from serious injury, but no one was safe outside the village.

The Hidatsa found ways of living with the weather and the Sioux, but they could not survive the smallpox epidemic of 1837. As a result, a way of life that had endured for many generations was almost completely destroyed. One man who lived through the epidemic became a well-known Hidatsa leader. Poor Wolf, also called Lean Wolf, had been born in Awatixa about 1820. When the epidemic struck the village, he contracted smallpox and was left alone in a lodge to die. During his illness he had a vision of a bear entering the lodge and approaching him. After he experienced this vision, Poor Wolf began to recover. The Hidatsa believed that the bear was a powerful healer and Poor Wolf took the bear as his spiritual protector. When he participated in ceremonies he wore anklets decorated with bear's teeth and carried a bear skull. With his strong spiritual protector Poor Wolf became a successful warrior, participated in many ceremonies, and eventually became a tribal leader.

Like Poor Wolf, other Hidatsa and Mandan survived the epidemic, but they had to rebuild their way of life. Around 1845, the Hidatsa abandoned their Knife River villages and moved up the Missouri to where the river made a sharp hooklike bend. Here they established a new village that they called Like-a-Fishhook. ▲

White Duck, a Hidatsa warrior, photographed by Edward S. Curtis about 1908.

LIKE-A-FISHHOOK
VILLAGE

Like-a-Fishhook Village was founded in the 1840s by a small group of Hidatsa and Mandan men, among them Poor Wolf and Missouri River, the keeper of the Hidatsa's most important sacred bundle. Missouri River walked clockwise around the village site four times and then prayed: "My gods, you are my protectors. Protect this village and I am sure it will stand long. Also, send rains that the gardens will grow. The children will grow up strong and healthy because my shrine is in the village."

Soon these first settlers were joined by other Hidatsa and Mandan. In 1862 another of the Hidatsa's allies, the Arikara, would abandon their overcrowded village near Fort Clark and come to live at Like-a-Fishhook. From the 1840s to the 1880s, Like-a-Fishhook would be the social, political, and commercial center of the Upper Missouri.

Non-Indian traders accompanied the Indians on their move up the Mis-

souri. Shortly after Like-a-Fishhook was settled, a trading company established Fort Berthold nearby as a trading post. For most of its existence, Like-a-Fishhook was known as Fort Berthold, and the latter name was later given to the Indian reservation designated for the Hidatsa, Mandan, and Arikara. Other trading posts soon sprang up around the village as well. These posts added to the non-Indian population of the area and encouraged its development as a commercial center.

In 1851, representatives of all the tribes of the northern Plains attended a treaty council at Fort Laramie. The treaty they signed there was an attempt to establish peaceful relations among the Indians by defining the boundaries of the territories claimed by the various tribes. The Indians were also promised trade goods if the tribes maintained peaceful relations. Although the Sioux and the Hidatsa both agreed to the treaty, hostilities between the two tra-

Fort Berthold trading post in 1865.

ditional enemies continued. As early as the 1830s the Hidatsa had asked the government for protection from the Sioux, but the U.S. Army could not spare the troops. It was not until 1862, when the Santee Sioux carried out numerous attacks against non-Indian settlers and traders, that the federal government agreed to provide military protection for the area. The government established several forts along the Missouri and in 1864 sent a cavalry company to Fort Berthold. The cavalry remained there until 1867 when, because of the poor condition of the buildings, it was relocated 18 miles downstream to the newly built Fort Stevenson.

Because the journey by steamboat up the Missouri was a relatively safe and comfortable one, numerous sportsmen, explorers, scientists, and artists made the trip to Like-a-Fishhook. Twenty or 30 steamboats docked at the

village every summer. The observations of these visitors, the journals of the traders, and the official government reports provide a detailed picture of life in Like-a-Fishhook. One observer was Henry Boller, a young Philadelphian who served as a clerk in one of the trading posts from 1858 to 1862. Boller used his diaries and letters home to write *Among the Indians*, a lighthearted book about his experiences.

U.S. government representatives, known as Indian agents, had been involved with the Hidatsa since the early 1800s. The agents were assigned to carry out federal policies toward the Indians and to distribute annuities, the yearly payments of money and provisions promised to the tribes in treaties. Tribes living along the Missouri River were given trade goods if they did not make war upon other Indians or non-Indians. As long as relations between the Hidatsa and other tribes were peaceful, Indian agents did little more than make brief visits to distribute guns, ammunition, clothing, food, and other annuities.

None of the agents had stayed long enough to have a significant impact on the Indians' way of life. In the 1860s the U.S. government initiated a new policy the goal of which was to promote peace between Indians and non-Indians and convince the Indians to adopt non-Indian ways. After that, agents became more intrusive. They were instructed to teach Indians how to be farmers and encourage them to convert to Christianity. The Office of Indian Affairs was the federal agency that oversaw the government's programs. In 1868 it ordered the Hidatsa Indian agent Mahlon Wilkinson either to take up permanent residence at Like-a-Fishhook or to resign as agent.

Wilkinson had been living more than 200 miles south of Like-a-Fishhook in what is now Yankton, South Dakota, and would visit the village once or twice a year. Now he moved into the deserted Fort Berthold and set up a formal administrative center there. It soon included a blacksmith shop, carpentry shop, sawmill, and gristmill. In 1875 a new agency was built a mile and a half away from the village. By 1880 the agency would consist of an issuehouse, where food, supplies, and other annuities were distributed, a meat house, a schoolhouse, a blacksmith and tin shop, a carpentry shop, an office, a wareroom, a toolhouse, a grain house,

An early photograph of Fort Berthold Agency, probably taken in the 1880s.

a hay barn, a gristmill, a sawmill, a boardinghouse, and five cottages that housed the people who worked for the agency.

In 1876 a Congregational mission was established at Fort Berthold. Missionaries had made regular visits to the village for some time, but no one had been willing to live there permanently until Reverend Charles L. Hall and his wife arrived that year. The Halls had met while he was the pastor at the Congregational church in Springfield, South Dakota, and she was teaching at the Santee Indian Mission School in Nebraska. The mission they built was a combination of church, school, and residence. They struggled to learn the Arikara, Mandan, and Hidatsa languages so they could converse directly with the Indians of Like-a-Fishhook. In the meantime, they spoke Dakota, the language of the Santee Sioux, to interpreters who translated their words into the appropriate languages.

Although the Indians now received trade goods from the outside world and the agents and missionaries made great efforts to get them to adopt non-Indian ways, they continued to follow most of their traditions. The Hidatsa, Mandan, and Arikara each occupied its own section of the village, established its own government, and followed its own religious practices. The various Indian agents at Fort Berthold believed that a log cabin would be a more practical home for each family than the earth lodges inhabited by extended families. However, most Indians preferred the companionship of the many relatives who lived in the same earth lodge. At first only a few families moved into log cabins that the government furnished with beds, tables and chairs, and other articles. But some of those who continued to live in earth lodges began using iron bedsteads.

In the early days of the village, the lodges had been set up in circles facing an open center. As the settlement be-

In 1872 Like-a-Fishhook was crowded with earth lodges, drying racks, and log cabins.

came more densely populated and people began to build log cabins for winter use, the open spaces gradually filled in, making for crowded, unsanitary conditions.

The Indians were reluctant to give up their earth lodges, but they did accept other changes encouraged by the agents and missionaries. As a result of the availability of manufactured goods, the crafts of pottery making, flint working, and mat making disappeared. The agents issued iron skillets, enamel teakettles, coffee pots, porcelain and ironstone dinnerware, and tin knives, forks, and spoons. Copper and iron cooking kettles, among the earliest trade goods, were not readily accepted because they imparted a metallic taste to the food and rusted easily, but as the Indians became used to these goods they overcame their initial reluctance to use them. The willow mats and hides the Indians had placed around the fireplace to sit upon were replaced by wooden benches.

Clothing, too, changed. The agents believed that when the Indians wore the same clothing as non-Indians they would more readily adopt non-Indian attitudes about work, school, and Christianity. Agents issued shoes, skirts, trousers, dresses, and petticoats as well as cloth for sewing their own garments in hopes of getting the Indians to give up their traditional hide clothing. The mission school taught girls how to sew so they could make the new styles for themselves and their

Although government agents encouraged Indian men to wear non-Indian clothing, most continued to wear the traditional hide shirts, leggings, and moccasins.

families. But the Indians did not completely accept the new fashions. The women sewed the agency-issued cloth into the same simple style of dress as they had earlier made from hides. The men continued to wear leggings of hide. Sometimes they cut a pair of government-issue trousers to make leggings. On special occasions they would wear a shirt made of hide or cloth. Moccasins remained the universally popular form of footwear. The men and women dressed for comfort rather than to please the agents. Only Indians who worked for the agents wore suits, and they changed into their traditional clothing as soon as they could.

The agents had even less success in changing the social and religious life of the villagers than they did with housing and clothing. The extended kinship system never disappeared, and clan membership continued to regulate family obligations and marriages. Both agents and missionaries abhorred the Indian practice of having more than one wife. However, one visitor who spent a winter at Like-a-Fishhook in the lodge of a man who had five wives reported favorably on the comfortable way of life for all members of the family because the women shared the work.

One attempt at change did meet with some success. Many men agreed to become farmers or wage earners and give up their extensive reliance on hunting. The various government treaties guaranteed seeds, plows, and agricultural instruction to the Indians who wanted to farm. Agents were told to provide every encouragement and assistance to these Indians. No one, however, gave much thought to the difficulties of large-scale farming on the Plains. Indian women had used the fertile floodplains for their small fields, but the government wanted the men to raise surplus crops to sell and encouraged farming on large plots away from the river. Year after year, the crops were stricken by drought, early frost, insects, and other disasters.

Two kinds of agriculture eventually evolved in Indian society: the simple, small-scale type practiced by Indian women, and the mechanical, large-scale type practiced by Indian men. The women continued to work their family plots and grow the basic crops of corn, squash, and beans, with a few new vegetables for variety. When potatoes and turnips were introduced, the Indians did not like them and would not dig the new crops out of the ground until the agent offered to buy them. As before, the women owned their crops and could sell or trade any surplus that was not needed by the family. They kept the money they made from their gardens and used it to purchase other food or any material goods that their families needed.

The men became more and more involved in farming large plots with whatever mechanical means were made available to them. In the 1871 *Annual Report* of the Office of Indian Affairs, the Indian agent John Tappen reported that the men had broken 640 acres in the floodplains and grown enough corn and squash to sustain the families for the winter. As a reward for their efforts, Tappen suggested that the men be given wagons and horse harnesses. The men also grew wheat and oats, but as the Indians did not eat these foods, the crops were turned over to the agent to be processed and sold. Any money the men earned from their farming was kept for them by the agent, who also controlled its disbursement.

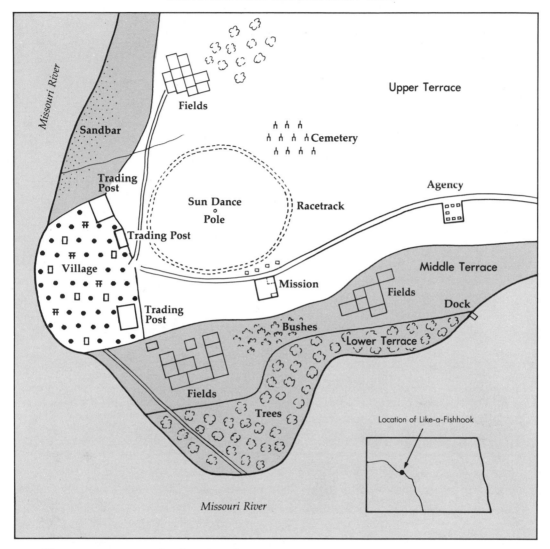

The men continued to hunt to obtain some of the family's meat. Although by the 1870s most of the buffalo had been killed off by non-Indian hunters, antelope, deer, elk, bear, beaver, rabbit, wild turkey, duck, geese, and other game were still plentiful. In addition beef and pork were regularly issued by the agent. Cattle, pigs, and chickens were introduced by traders and agents, but very few Indians raised them because they required a lot of care.

One of the first non-Indian concepts to gain the acceptance of the Indians was that of wage labor. Traders hired Indian men to hunt and trap and Indian women to cook and sew. The U.S. military also paid Indian men to scout and hunt. The Office of Indian Affairs stressed that hiring the Indians was a way to teach them money management and work etiquette. The first agency jobs the Indians held were those of interpreter and general helper, but more opportunities developed as the agency grew. In 1874 the agent at Fort Berthold reported that 40 Indian men were working steadily as clerks, blacksmiths, and in other trades. To encourage wage labor the agents withheld certain goods from annuities and used them as incentives. Only those Indians who earned wages through work could acquire such luxury items as sugar and coffee.

To encourage the spread of Christianity, the Office of Indian Affairs authorized the Indian agents to punish people who participated in traditional religious ceremonies. Men who followed their traditional beliefs were jailed or, even worse, had their hair cut off. Hidatsa men wore their hair long and cutting it off was viewed as a personal violation. Cutting a man's hair also made him appear more like a non-Indian. The Hidatsa, however, never really gave up their practices; they just became secretive about them. They continued to observe the Naxpike and the Buffalo Calling Ceremony and other rituals, and men still sought spiritual protectors in the traditional manner.

The efforts of missionaries and agents did eventually result in some converts to Christianity. One of the first was Poor Wolf, the second most important chief of the Hidatsa. A successful warrior and hunter, Poor Wolf had helped found Like-a-Fishhook and was a respected political and religious leader. He had participated in negotiating a number of important treaties with the U.S. government. As a young man Poor Wolf had scorned non-Indian ways, but later in life he allowed his daughters to go away to a mission boarding school. When they returned, they asked him to become a Christian. It was a difficult decision because accepting Christianity would mean giving up all his old beliefs and sacred objects. "Must I give up all the old songs, which are a part of the life of our people?" he asked. "Must I give up the charms that I have carried on my person for years and which I believe have defended me from evil influence? My body is tattooed to show my allegiance to various spirits. Can I cut these out of my flesh?"

When Poor Wolf did decide to become a Christian he threw away all his religious objects. Other members of the tribe called him foolish and said he would suffer sad consequences. He became blind, his wife was crippled, and his team of horses was killed by lightning, but he stayed with his new faith. Eventually he partially regained his eyesight and his wife recovered from her paralysis. Most Indians who converted found giving up their traditional beliefs less of an ordeal. Others simply did not convert and never gave up their traditional beliefs and practices.

Education brought about many changes in Indian culture. The first school had been established by the agency in 1870, but it attracted little interest and closed soon afterward. In 1873 another day school was opened at the agency. This school struggled along for several years and when Reverend Hall's mission school opened in 1877 competed with it for students. In accordance with traditional child-rearing methods, Indian children were allowed to decide for themselves which school to attend and even whether to attend school at all. Edward Goodbird, a Hidatsa man who grew up in Like-a-Fishhook, remembered going to the mission school during the mornings but not at-

Poor Wolf, the Hidatsa chief whose daughters convinced him to accept Christianity, and his family, photographed about 1905.

Crow-Flies-High, the leader of the band of Indians that left Like-a-Fishhook in 1870.

tending during the afternoons in order to play or attend dances. Once when he did not receive the gift he wanted at a Christmas party at the mission school, he decided to go to the agency school for a while. The curriculum was similar at both schools: English, mathematics, and geography for all students; agriculture and manual skills for boys; and cooking, sewing, and other domestic skills for girls.

While they were struggling with the new demands being made on them, most of the Indians at Like-a-Fishhook probably did not think about the effect these changes would have on their fu-

ture. Federal officials, however, were very aware of the long-term changes planned for the three tribes. One change, however, was particularly obvious: the reduction in the size of their territory.

The 1851 Treaty of Fort Laramie had recognized more than 12 million acres as the hunting territory of the 3 tribes. Government officials argued that this area was too large, and in 1866 the tribes agreed to accept an area of eight million acres, which was set aside as an official reservation. This treaty was never ratified by Congress. However, in 1870 President Ulysses S. Grant signed an executive order establishing Fort Berthold Reservation on this land. In 1880, at the request of Frederick Billings, the president of the Northern Pacific Railroad (who wanted the land for his railroad), another executive order reduced the size of the reservation to less than three million acres. An investigation preceding the 1880 executive order indicated that the three tribes used the land as hunting grounds and for their winter villages, but other officials had argued that the tribes were not using the area.

There were some Hidatsa who struggled to maintain their traditional way of life. In 1870 a group took action in the traditional way: They left the village and moved 120 miles upriver to build a new community outside the boundaries of the reservation. Although the decision to leave Like-a-Fishhook was the result of many minor occurrences, the incident that brought about the move was a disagreement between the war chief Crow-Flies-High and the government-supported leaders Poor Wolf and Crow Paunch over who should be chief of the Hidatsa. According to some reports, Poor Wolf and Crow Paunch threatened to assassinate Crow-Flies-High, the leader of the group that eventually moved away, because he complained to the agent about the two chiefs' failure to distribute rations they had been given.

The reasons for leaving Like-a-Fishhook were soon forgotten, but the reasons for staying away were obvious. Indians living within the reservation boundaries were pressured to send their children to school, become farmers, and follow the laws of the Court of Indian Offenses. The Court of Indian Offenses, run by the Office of Indian Affairs, punished Indians for having more than one wife and for participating in dances and traditional religious ceremonies. Off the reservation, people followed their ancestral ways, supporting themselves by cutting wood, tending small gardens, and acting as scouts for the U.S. Army. The agents at Fort Berthold thought Crow-Flies-High's band was a bad influence on the residents of Like-a-Fishhook because it was

a constant reminder that people did not have to agree to live according to the government's ideas.

After years of pressure from the agency to return to the reservation, Crow-Flies-High and his followers moved back in 1894. By then, however, the rest of the Hidatsa, Mandan, and Arikara had moved away from Like-a-Fishhook and settled elsewhere on the reservation. The various Indian agents had for a long time supported the idea of establishing communities on other parts of the reservation, but it was not until the 1880s that any Indians acted on the idea. By 1882 Like-a-Fishhook was overcrowded and in decline. The buffalo were gone, the timber resources were depleted, and the people needed more land for farming. Moreover, peace had come to the valley so the people did not need the protection of the stockaded village. That year 20 families moved 20 miles upriver, where they established a new community at Elbowoods. With the aid of government workers and machinery, land was cleared and the people turned to making a living as farmers. Other families soon followed. By 1888 Like-a-Fishhook was deserted except for a few elders who refused to leave. ▲

A Hidatsa woman, photographed by Edward S. Curtis about 1908.

ALLOTMENT
AND
ADAPTATION

Leaving Like-a-Fishhook was not easy. Although the agency was located at Elbowoods on the east side of the Missouri River, most of the people moved to the west side, where they were more removed from the agent's influence. There were no roads on the west side. No bridge spanned the river; wagons had to be dismantled and floated across. Horses swam across. New houses had to be built. Edward Goodbird remembered camping in a tipi while he and his father built a log cabin. It took them a month to put up the walls, spread clay over them, and cover the roof with willows, grass, and sod. Goodbird's family had moved too late in the season to plant a garden, so they gathered food from the surroundings that winter.

The agents had hoped the Indians would establish individual farmsteads spread out over the reservation, but the people settled in small communities along the river. Families chose to settle in areas where they had previously wintered or hunted. Various riverside communities settled by clan or extended family groups sprang up. Families related to the Hidatsa leader Small Ankle settled west of the Missouri near a steep-sloped hill with a flat top, or butte, that would become the town of Independence, North Dakota. People related to the Mandan elders Bad Gun and Crows Heart also established settlements on the west bank of the Missouri. The Arikara remained on the east side of the river, where they established the community of Nishu.

Not only was it hard for the Indians to rebuild their houses, but it was also hard to give up the noise and bustle of Like-a-Fishhook. Friends were now separated by long distances. More than 60 years after the abandonment of Like-a-Fishhook, Paul Hanna, a student at the University of North Dakota, interviewed former residents and found many who still regretted the move. One

Because there was no bridge across the Missouri River, the Indians had to use ferries when they moved their households from Like-a-Fishhook to smaller, scattered communities.

old man explained that at Like-a-Fishhook food was shared and everyone helped each other, but that after the move it was more difficult for people to get together. Ceremonies could no longer be held so easily because of the time it took to travel from one village to another. People had to deal with hardships on their own and suffered loneliness.

Each new community needed schools and churches as well as houses, barns, and other farm buildings. The government established small day schools and provided a teacher and housekeeper, usually a husband and wife, to teach all grades and run the school. The Congregational church helped set up places where services could be held, but missionaries seldom wanted to stay in the isolated communities. The church solved this problem by training residents of the communities to be preachers. In 1904 Edward Goodbird became the first Hidatsa to take up the post of assistant missionary.

Because of the distance between most villages and the new agency at

Elbowoods, government stations were built closer to the communities so that people would not have to travel so far to receive the distributions of food and other goods to which they were entitled. Most communities also had several small general stores that were operated by Indians. One of the most popular stores was operated by Wolf Chief. He had been a buffalo hunter and warrior but adapted to changing times by learning to read and write. Because Wolf Chief was a kind man and a good storyteller, people enjoyed shopping at his store.

Shortly after people began to leave Like-a-Fishhook, Congress passed the General Allotment Act of 1887. Its goal was to end the Indians' tribal rights to reservation land by making landowners of individual Indians. Under this act, reservations were to be divided into standardized plots, and each plot was to be given, or allotted, to a tribal member. Any land that was not allotted was to be sold and the proceeds used to support the tribe's educational and health needs. Thus, non-Indians would be able to buy land that had belonged to Indians by tradition and treaties. Congress recognized that many Indians had not yet had enough experience in managing land, and so the act provided that Indians could not sell their allotted lands for 25 years or until they demonstrated financial responsibility.

The Hidatsa, Mandan, and Arikara were all affected by the General Allotment Act. An executive order of 1891 specifically provided for the allotment

Wolf Chief's hospitality and lively conversation attracted customers to his general store at Independence, North Dakota.

of the Fort Berthold Reservation. Unlike the allotment of most reservations, the 1891 executive order restricted the sale of unallotted lands and reserved them for future members of the tribe. Before the reservation could be allotted, the land had to be surveyed. The survey showed that the agency was outside the reservation boundary. As a result, President Benjamin Harrison restored 23,000 acres to the reservation in 1892.

Allotment of Fort Berthold Reservation lands began in 1894. Nearly 1,000 people were given plots of land.

Heads of families received 160 acres each. Women and men over the age of 18 who were not heads of families were given 80 acres per person. Children received 40 acres each. Every person was assigned an allotment number and allowed to select a plot. Family members tried to select land near each other so they could combine the plots into a single large tract, but that was not always possible. More often a family ended up with tracts several miles apart; they usually would live on one tract and hunt and farm on the others or lease the land to non-Indians. Children who later received allotments from the reserved lands almost never got plots near their family's other tracts.

Most of the residents of the various communities chose plots in or near the town in which they lived. Land along the river was allotted, but a large section of rugged land on the west side was not divided, and it became an open range for cattle grazing. The northeastern quarter of the reservation was reserved for future members of the tribe. As early as 1901 the idea of selling the reserved lands was proposed by the agents, but nothing was done until 1910 when Congress voted to open this land for sale to non-Indians, an action that violated the agreement of 1891. The Indians were vehemently opposed to selling the land, but the government persisted and eventually the tribes agreed to the sale. But some reservation leaders were still unhappy with the idea of selling reservation lands. They wrote

to Robert G. Valentine, the commissioner of Indian affairs, "They have got us now to our homes. That is the only thing we have now to protect. The land has been taken away and we have only to defend our homes."

The allotment and sale of reservation lands did lasting damage to the reservation's economic and political integrity. Allotment plots had been determined without regard to the varying types and features of the land. Many allotments were on land that was not suitable for farming, or the size of the plots was too small for large-scale agriculture. In the early days of allotment, the agents continued to encourage Indians to take up farming, but they later realized that ranching was better suited to Indian interests and to the land and climate. The west side of the reservation, designated as pastureland, was very rough and dry, and even 320 acres of grazing land—which was often the combined acreage of a family's allotment tracts—would not provide sufficient pasture for a large herd.

The General Allotment Act resulted in a problem that came to be known as fractionated heirship. Unlike the Hidatsa, who set aside land for future generations, Indians on most reservations did not reserve land for future residents. The General Allotment Act provided that, when an original allottee died, the land was to be divided equally among his or her heirs. Within a few generations, several hundred people would have legal claims to a piece of an allotment, and one person would have claims to pieces of more than one allotment. After the government opened the Hidatsa's reserved lands for sale to non-Indians in 1910, the tribe also faced the issue of fractionated heirship. The division of allotments would eventually cause friction among tribal members and sometimes involve families in court battles as well as intense personal struggles for ownership. The disputed land was often sold; it was easier to distribute money than fractions of an acre to the heirs.

In the early 1900s, however, most Indians on Fort Berthold Reservation were more concerned with making a living than with the eventual effects of fractionated heirship. By this time, everyone lived in log cabins or wooden frame houses much like any other northern Plains home, furnished with goods available through mail-order catalogs. Men dressed like non-Indian ranchers in blue jeans, cotton shirts, and cowboy boots. Most women wore the same type of clothing as their non-Indian counterparts, although some older women continued to wear the old-style calico dresses and shawls that were typical of the late 1800s. Educated Indians living in towns and cities dressed like their peers in non-Indian society. But although most Indians understood English, they preferred to speak the Hidatsa language.

The Hidatsa received rations of food as part of the annuities promised them in treaties with the U.S. government. When they collected their weekly rations, each family had to present a ticket, which was punched to indicate that the food had been distributed.

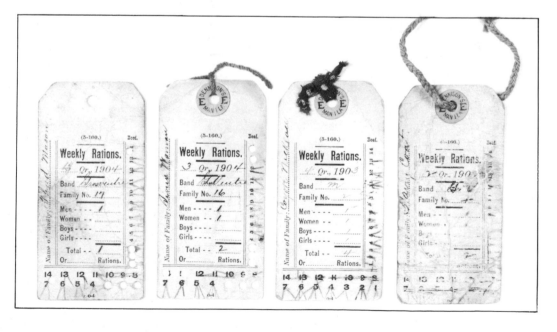

The Indians continued to observe their traditional ceremonies by holding them on American holidays. Often occasions such as this Fourth of July celebration in 1918 were really disguised Indian dances.

The men were primarily involved in growing crops and raising cattle. Like other farmers in the region, the Indians harvested their crops with mechanical reapers and carted the grain to the nearest railroad for shipment to a central market. Ranchers took their cattle to St. Paul or Chicago by rail. Some men who had attended off-reservation boarding schools were employed by the agency as teachers, clerks, interpreters, blacksmiths, and carpenters.

The presence of non-Indians in and near the communities exposed the Indians to American ideas about voting and led some of them to become interested in local politics. In 1902 several of the men served as delegates to the county Republican convention. In 1910

members of the Hidatsa, Mandan, and Arikara formed a business committee to represent the tribes to the agent, the federal government, and local governments. The 10-member committee carried out the business of the tribe, making decisions on government programs that affected the Indians and on matters concerning the land and its resources. The original committee members were selected by the elders of the tribes. As these representatives died or left the committee, the other committee members selected new representatives from among the tribe. Four of the original representatives were Hidatsa, among them Drags Wolf, the son of Crow-Flies-High, who had replaced his father as a reservation leader.

Indian women, particularly the elderly, did not take up the ways of non-Indian society as quickly as the men. Their primary concern was still the family. They continued to tend gardens, preserve food, sew clothing, and keep house. Some educated women worked for the agency as teachers, housekeepers, and field matrons, women who went into the homes of other Indians to teach modern methods of cooking, canning, and housekeeping.

As separate, widely dispersed communities sprang up, schools were built to meet the educational needs of the Indians. In each community and at Elbowoods, where the agency and Congregational mission were located, there were day schools operated by the Bureau of Indian Affairs, formerly the Office of Indian Affairs. Most students who attended the mission school were boarders, but day students were also accepted. Some students also attended off-reservation boarding schools in Bismarck and Wahpeton. Each of these schools offered a mixture of academic subjects such as reading, English, and mathematics, and vocational subjects such as cooking, sewing, and agriculture, all of which stressed non-Indian attitudes and values.

Although the agents continued to prohibit Indian dances and other traditional celebrations, many Indians got around the ban by adapting their ceremonies to the dominant society's calendar. Agents were pleased at how quickly the Indians of Fort Berthold Reservation organized Fourth of July celebrations. Upon closer scrutiny, however, these celebrations were really traditional dances made to look like non-Indian affairs for the benefit of the agent. Christmas became a time for the Indians' traditional giveaway ceremonies because that was when the agents permitted gift-giving. At this time members of the tribe gave gifts to those people who had in some way helped them achieve a goal or honor. On Decoration Day (Memorial Day), clan relatives carried out their traditional burial duties by weeding and decorating the graves of their deceased members.

From the time they had aided the Army as scouts against the Sioux, the Hidatsa, Mandan, and Arikara had always fought on the side of the United States. When the country entered World War I in 1917, some Hidatsa men enlisted and served in all branches of the armed forces. Those who remained at home bought war bonds, grew victory gardens to contribute food to the war effort, and celebrated with Victory Dances when the war was over.

In 1930 the Court of Claims ordered the federal government to compensate the Hidatsa, Mandan, and Arikara for the land removed from their reservation by the executive orders of 1870 and 1880. The tribes had argued for years that the government had treated them unfairly by withdrawing more than 11 million acres from Fort Berthold Reservation without paying the Indians anything for their loss of land and resources. When the agreement was reached in 1930, the Indians were awarded almost $5 million, of which nearly $3 million was deducted as payment for education, roads, health care, and other services the tribes had received from the government. The remainder was divided among all the members of the tribes, with each person receiving a little more than $1,000. Money due to any person under 18 years of age was deposited in a trust fund administered by the agent.

Many families used the settlement money to build new houses or remodel existing ones. Others bought farm machinery or added to their livestock. A few greedy local merchants extended credit to Indians and then wanted the agent to force these people to pay their bills immediately. The agent refused to intervene, and the Indians were free to spend their payments as they wished.

The technological changes that occurred in the first part of the 20th century also affected the Indians on Fort Berthold Reservation. Telephones, improved roads, and automobiles made communication among the various communities easier. A hospital was opened at Elbowoods in 1930. In 1934, Four Bears bridge was built just south of Elbowoods, connecting the east and west banks of the Missouri and making visits among communities easier.

New roads and new schools also brought a semblance of prosperity to the reservation, but many of these were built as part of relief programs designed to alleviate the economic depression of the 1930s. The settlement money from the U.S. government helped to offset the early effects of the depression among the Hidatsa. Eventually, however, the depression, coupled with a drought that turned the Plains into a dust bowl in the early 1930s, affected the Indians, too. Many had leased their land to non-Indian ranchers and farmers. When the crops failed and there was no market for cattle, the lessees had no money with which to pay the rent due the Indian landowners. The Bureau of Indian Affairs made arrangements for the lessees to pay the rent in crops or cattle instead of cash, but the Indians were unable to sell these goods and were desperately short of money. In 1934 the crops failed completely. Drags Wolf and Adlai Stevenson (not the American politician but a member of Crow-Flies-High's band) wrote to North Dakota congressman James H. Sinclair asking for help. Eventually members of the tribe were employed to build roads, construct dams, and dig wells as part of several relief projects.

Despite the continuing efforts of agents and missionaries to convince the Indians to give up their traditional ways, people continued to respect the sacred bundles of their clans. In 1933, members of the Waterbuster clan sought to regain possession of the Waterbuster sacred bundle. After its Hidatsa keeper had accepted Christianity, it had been sold in 1907 to George G. Heye, who would later found the Museum of the American Indian in New York City. Although tribal members had been upset about its sale, they decided to wait until after the man who sold the bundle died to make a formal request for its return. After several years of negotiation the bundle was exchanged for a sacred buffalo medicine horn and returned to the tribe. The members of the Waterbuster clan maintained that the severe drought of the 1930s had been caused by the absence of the bundle. After its return in 1938, there was so much rain that some suggested sending the bundle back to Heye.

During the 1930s there was a major change in federal Indian policy. In reaction to the loss of traditional ways and the demise of tribal governments caused by the General Allotment Act, Congress passed the Indian Reorgani-

zation Act (IRA) in 1934. This act was intended to prevent the further loss of reservation lands and strengthen tribal governments. The IRA halted the sale of reservation lands and gave each tribe the right to establish its own constitutional government, with elected representatives, and to incorporate as a business. Once incorporated, the tribe could borrow money, hire its own employees, and carry out business on its own behalf. Previously, agents had controlled all the tribe's money and had made all the decisions concerning tribal relations with the state and federal governments. As a result, the members of the tribe had had little power. Although the business committee organized in

Four Bears Bridge, built across the Missouri River in 1934, helped connect the widely dispersed Indian communities.

The costume worn by a participant in the grass dance, a traditional Indian dance, drawn by Edward Goodbird in 1914. By the mid-1900s many traditions of the Hidatsa had been replaced by non-Indian customs.

1910 was still operating, it acted mainly in an advisory capacity to government officials.

Before any tribe could be included in the programs set forth by the IRA, it first had to approve the act. In 1934, the Indians of Fort Berthold overwhelmingly approved the IRA and set about drawing up a tribal constitution. The former business committee served as a model for the new governing body, called the tribal council. In addition, the Bureau of Indian Affairs provided examples of constitutions for the Indians

to follow. The Hidatsa, Mandan, and Arikara officially designated themselves the Three Affiliated Tribes and incorporated as a business.

The constitution drawn up by the Indians stipulated the requirements for membership in the Three Affiliated Tribes and provided rules for the election of its officials. The original requirements have been revised through the years to reflect changes in national and tribal policies. Today Indians must have one-quarter or more Hidatsa, Mandan, or Arikara ancestry to belong to the Three Tribes. Any member who is 18 years or older and resides on the reservation can vote in tribal elections. Representatives from each of the reservation's five districts are elected to the tribal council for two-year terms. A chairman elected by the members of the tribe heads the council.

The Three Affiliated Tribes were the only North Dakota Indians to approve the IRA. For the first few years, however, the tribal council had little business to conduct and continued to act mainly as advisers to the agent. But as the Three Tribes' territory became the focus of increasing interest to the U.S. government, which wanted to build a series of dams along the Missouri River, the council would play a major role in negotiations over matters that threatened most of the Indians' agricultural land as well as their communities.

U. S. participation in World War II brought a measure of prosperity to the Three Tribes as the demand for grain increased and crops sold for high prices. Some Indians served overseas in the war while others helped on the home front. Skilled and educated men and women moved to urban areas to do factory work in war-related industries. Indian dances were held to raise funds for the war effort. When the soldiers returned home at war's end, they were honored with Victory Dances.

The first half of the 20th century brought many changes to the Hidatsa culture. With the presence of non-Indians the reservation was less isolated from the rest of the world. The Hidatsa selected the objects and ideas of non-Indian technology and culture that were useful to their way of life. Some Hidatsa who had been born at Like-a-Fishhook and raised in the traditional ways of the tribe worried that younger members were losing their heritage. However, neither the Hidatsa who held onto the old ways nor those who adopted new ones were prepared to deal with the changes that would be brought about by Garrison Dam. ▲

Bears Belly, photographed by Edward S. Curtis about 1908.

GARRISON DAM
AND THE
RESERVATION TODAY

Of all the changes endured by the Hidatsa, the most disastrous was the construction of Garrison Dam and the subsequent flooding of their ancient homelands. Throughout their moves from the Knife River villages to Like-a-Fishhook and then to smaller communities, the Indians had maintained their orientation to the river. The rich bottomlands continued to be used for farming, and the river itself linked the towns on its banks. But the source of life of the Three Tribes was not viewed so favorably by others.

Often called Big Muddy, the Missouri River presented hazards to navigation and challenges to life and property. The floods that replenished the fields of the Three Tribes threatened downstream cities and crops. Floods had taken lives and carried away property for generations. As early as 1838, the army had tried to improve navigation by removing dead trees from the river. Later, Congress voted to increase

the Missouri's use in navigation by providing funds to deepen some sections of the river.

The idea of controlling the river with dams arose in the 1920s. By that time ways had been developed to use water power to produce electricity, and the growing demand for hydroelectric power joined the needs for unimpeded navigation and flood control. In 1940, the Fort Peck Dam, at Fort Peck, Montana, was built, becoming the first dam on the Missouri and the first earth-filled dam in the world. Several smaller dams were also constructed on the larger tributaries of the Missouri. Even with these measures, however, flooding continued.

A flood in the early spring of 1943 caused more than $50 million in damage to some areas of the Missouri Valley. People who suffered losses in the flooding demanded relief, and members of Congress from the affected states asked for some form of flood control. In May of that year the House Flood Committee directed the U.S. Army Corps of Engineers to draw up a flood control plan for the Missouri River. Colonel Lewis A. Pick, an engineer from Omaha, Nebraska, one of the cities frequently hit by floods, was placed in charge of the project.

The proposal devised by Pick, known as the Missouri River Basin Plan, called for protective levees, or ridges of earth along the river, five dams on the Missouri itself, and seven additional dams on its tributaries. There were objections to the proposal even before it was submitted to Congress. The Bureau of Reclamation, a division of the Department of the Interior, objected that the Army Corps of Engineers was asserting authority over waterways managed by the bureau. It ordered William Glenn Sloan, an engineer with the bureau, to draw up an alternative plan. The Three Affiliated Tribes also objected: Pick's plan, if carried out, would submerge thousands of

Big Muddy, the Missouri River, as it wends its way through North Dakota.

acres of the reservation's rich bottom-land under a reservoir created by one of the dams. In 1943 the council passed a resolution opposing any dam that would adversely affect the reservation.

Sloan's alternative plan emphasized irrigation in conjunction with the construction of many smaller dams along the tributaries of the Missouri. Three major dams on the Missouri were to be combined with canals to carry reservoir water to drought-stricken areas of the Dakotas.

A third organization, the Missouri Valley Authority, submitted a plan that gained more public and congressional support than the first two proposals. This plan combined the region's irrigation and flood control needs with its need for electricity. The dams would be operated by companies as profit-making enterprises, rather than by the government. The Army Corps of Engineers and the Interior's Bureau of Reclamation feared their plans would lose congressional approval. Together they drew up a compromise, the Pick-Sloan Plan, named for the leaders of the two projects. This plan called for five major dams on the Missouri: Garrison Dam in North Dakota and Oahe, Big Bend, Fort Randall, and Gavins Point dams in South Dakota. The Pick-Sloan plan was rushed through Congress and approved by President Franklin D. Roosevelt in 1944. Although there is no evidence that the proponents of the plan deliberately chose Indian land, more than 550 square miles of tribal land in North and South Dakota were eventually flooded, and 23 tribes were affected by the dams. The most severe damage was suffered by the Three Affiliated Tribes.

Not one of the flood control plans considered the tribal treaty rights or Indian water rights covered by the Winters Doctrine. The Winters Doctrine resulted from a 1907 Supreme Court case in which the Fort Belknap Indians of Montana sued a farmer to prevent him from damming the Milk River that flowed through their reservation. The court ruled that Indians have a right to sufficient water to meet their needs, a right that can never be taken away. The construction of Garrison Dam began before either the Bureau of Indian Affairs or local tribal officials became aware that it would cause massive flooding and loss of the Indians' land. In 1947 the Bureau of Indian Affairs instituted a series of studies to determine the potential impact of the dam on the Three Tribes. That same year the Indians sent a committee to Washington to protest the dam. The Army Corps of Engineers planned to take the Three Tribes' land by eminent domain, the right of the government to appropriate private property for public projects. In response, the Indians argued that the 1851 Treaty of Fort Laramie stated the land could not be taken without tribal and congressional approval. Congress supported the Indians and halted all dam construction until the jurisdictional issues were settled.

Indians attempt to salvage valuable wood before the area is flooded by Lake Sakakawea, the reservoir created by Garrison Dam.

Neither the Army Corps of Engineers nor the Indians were willing to compromise, and negotiations dragged on for more than a year. In 1947 the Three Tribes accepted a settlement of more than $5 million, with a provision that they could petition for an additional sum in compensation for losses not covered in the settlement. In 1949 the Three Tribes were awarded another $7.5 million. The total compensation, however, was more than $9 million less than the amount that had been recommended by a private appraisal company hired by the Three Tribes.

Regardless of the amount, no sum could repay the heartache caused by the flooding of the Indians' land and the removal of people from their communities. Many Indian people were still following traditional ways of life, as the surveys conducted before the construction of the dam showed. The dam would disrupt every aspect of their daily lives. On the land that was to be flooded the women raised corn, potatoes, and other vegetables in household gardens, and the men hunted and ranched. The timber along the river provided wood for fuel and houses and was sold as fence posts. The trees sheltered livestock and game animals; they were, as one man said, "as good as a barn." Outcrops of lignite coal also provided fuel. Although most people got water from the Missouri River, streams, wells, and springs also provided water. Relatives continued to live near each other. The strong extended family meant that everyone shared the available resources. The Indians believed the land, water, trees, and other natural resources belonged to no one person and were for all the people to use. When questioned about their future, people could not imagine life without the resources of the river and assumed that after the dam was built their lives would be the same.

The construction of Garrison Dam was completed in 1956. The tribes lost much more than the 155,000 acres of rich farmland covered by Lake Sakakawea, the reservoir. All the communities and most of the homes—90 percent of the families—had to be moved out of the flood zone. Most land away from the river was already owned by non-Indians, and it was not easy for the people to find a new place to live. Members of the Three Tribes had to take whatever land was available, which meant that they were unable to reconstitute the family-oriented communities in which they had lived.

Individual families scattered across the dry windy uplands of the reservation. Much of the available land—land that no one had wanted before—was rough and unsuitable for farming or ranching. Because the settlement money did not cover the cost of building new houses, the Indians' old ones had to be moved, and many suffered irreparable cracks along the way. Two hundred thirty miles of new roads had to be built. Extending roads and water pipelines to the Indians' scattered houses would take more than 30 years. All seven day schools had to be rebuilt, and every child on the reservation had to change schools. The reservation hospital at Elbowoods was never rebuilt. Five church cemeteries, 27 private burial grounds, and a special cemetery for those Indians who had served as scouts for the U.S. Army were removed to higher ground. The Four Bears bridge

A house is moved out of the flood zone of Lake Sakakawea to a new site on higher ground.

south of Elbowoods was moved to the north end of the reservoir. The lack of other bridges, however, made some parts of the reservation more isolated than before. The river that had connected the people now divided them.

Residents and businesses of what were formerly Sanish, Van Hook, and Elbowoods relocated to New Town, the largest town in the area and the site of the new Indian agency. At the time the Indians moved there, New Town was not on the reservation and was primar-

ily a non-Indian community. The Indians resented having the agency located off the reservation and later built their own offices for the tribal council and other tribal activities on the reservation on the west side of the reservoir.

People living in the Arikara community of Nishu resettled to the town of White Shield. The former Mandan communities of Red Buttes and Charging Eagle were consolidated into Twin Buttes. The new community of Man-

An office building built in 1978 on the west side of Lake Sakakawea is the administrative center for the Three Affiliated Tribes.

daree was established, taking its name from all three tribes whose members might live there: *Man* from the Mandan, *da* from the Hidatsa, and *Ree*, the name by which the Arikara were familiarly known. Most of those who moved to Mandaree were from the former Hidatsa communities of Independence and Shell Creek.

Other difficulties arose as a result of the dam. The Three Affiliated Tribes had always been divided into warring factions. Opposing groups disagreed on the political direction the tribe should take—whether it should try to preserve its Indian heritage or take on the values of non-Indian society. The arguments that ensued over how to fight the construction of the dam and then how to spend the settlement money created even more division between the groups. The tribal chairman, Martin Cross, and his supporters believed that the money should be divided evenly among all the tribal members. Carl Whitman, Jr., the leader of the opposition party, proposed that the money be put into a tribal fund and used to develop the resources of the reservation. The reorganization of the tribal government to reflect new districts led to further dissension. When Martin Cross was reelected tribal chairman in 1952, Carl Whitman, Jr., had been disqualified because he now lived in a different district than the one in which he ran. Whitman wrote to the secretary of the interior, the United States attorney general, the commis-

sioner of Indian affairs, and local officials protesting that the election was unfair because others who had moved out of their districts had been allowed to run in their old district. Whitman asked that Cross's victory be overturned, but he was unsuccessful. Because of a delay in approving the reorganization there was no tribal election in 1954. As a result Cross served a four-year term. In 1956, however, Whitman was elected tribal chairman.

In addition to these two major factions, others surfaced over the years, and people could not agree on matters pertaining to the reservation. A 1972 report by the Economic Development Administration described reservation politics as unusually divisive. It also noted that people still seemed to lack a common goal.

There is no doubt that the Hidatsa, Mandan, and Arikara found it difficult to adjust to the changes brought on by Garrison Dam. The biggest change was in family income. When they had lived in the bottomlands people had supplemented their cash incomes with foods produced by gardening and hunting as well as with free fuel from the local coal and the trees along the river. Now these resources were unavailable, and the Indians were more dependent on earnings from paid work. But very few jobs were available in rural North Dakota. The number of people on welfare increased from one percent before relocation in 1956 to nine percent in 1960. Many of the housing improvements

Irrigation pipes on Fort Berthold Reservation. Improved methods of irrigation resulting from government programs begun in the late 1960s increased the productivity of the Indians' arid farmland.

promised during the dam negotiations, such as electricity, wells, and indoor plumbing, were slow in coming. In 1966, 90 percent of the housing was still run-down and lacked indoor plumbing.

The desperate situation of the Indians attracted the attention of several federal agencies. As a result, several government-sponsored programs were initiated on the reservation in the late 1960s. The Indians received housing improvements through federal building programs. The Public Health Service awarded a grant to drill wells and install septic tanks for some homes. The Economic Development Administration provided funds to build several tribal

offices and a tourist complex known as Four Bears resort.

Federal and tribal efforts to attract industry to the reservation were not very successful. Industries that opened, such as the Venride Corporation, a manufacturer of amusement-park rides, and the Three Tribes Stoneware, which sold pottery made out of local clay, were short-lived or employed only a few people. The settlement of several claims cases in the 1970s was the major boost to the Indians' economy. The Three Tribes had sued the federal government for insufficient payment for lands sold to non-Indians. In November 1976 each tribal member received

$1,229.86 as his or her share of the settlement.

Today the Hidatsa's way of life is much like that of other rural westerners. They live in modern ranch-style houses, dress in blue jeans and cowboy boots, eat hamburgers at fast-food restaurants, and attend church on Sunday. Most homes have television sets, many with satellite dishes to improve reception. A tribal newspaper and radio station keep residents up-to-date on Indian issues. As it has for most rural westerners, the pickup truck has replaced the horse. People drive many miles for shopping, doctor's appointments, and social events.

Most Hidatsa speak English, but they may also speak Hidatsa or study it in school. Depending on where they live some of the children attend schools funded by the Bureau of Indian Affairs. Others attend public schools on the reservation. There are a few differences in curriculum between the two. Both fulfill the state curriculum requirements, but the tribally-run schools offer classes in tribal history and language and are more oriented toward traditional culture. Often they are staffed by Indian

The Mandaree school, funded by the Bureau of Indian Affairs, serves Indian children from the community of Mandaree.

teachers. A tribally chartered community college provides postsecondary education in liberal arts and vocational skills. Graduates of the tribal high school and community college often go on to other colleges in the region. Many members of the Three Tribes have earned college degrees and returned to the reservation to work as teachers, social workers, nurses, and administrators. Hidatsa students who need financial aid to finance their education must apply for it from the same sources as non-Indians. The Three Tribes and the Bureau of Indian Affairs also award scholarships to outstanding students.

Studies have shown that Indians suffer higher rates of diabetes and certain other health problems than non-Indians. The Indian Health Service, a health-care program funded by the federal government, operates clinics on the reservation to treat minor ailments. For more serious problems the Indians must seek treatment at off-reservation hospitals because there is no reservation hospital. The lack of hospital facilities means that people have to drive many miles for treatment. For this reason tribal leaders have asked that a hospital be built on the reservation to replace the one at Elbowoods that was destroyed by the flooding.

The reservation has a variety of churches of different denominations. Most Hidatsa are Christians, although they may also follow some traditional Indian religious beliefs and practices. Many Indians do not see a need to sep-

arate their traditional practices from those of Christianity and maintain that all ways of worshiping are appropriate. They believe that if a spirit quest can help a young person achieve psychological security, then such practices should be encouraged. Likewise, if a sacred bundle can help an ill elder feel better, then using it in traditional ways cannot be wrong.

Like many tribes today, the Hidatsa hold powwows and other dances. A powwow is a social event at which the people camp in temporary shelters, perform traditional dances, and visit among each other. The various Indian communities on the reservation have permanent powwow grounds where they hold powwows every summer. During the winter, smaller powwows are held in community centers or school gymnasiums. These events are sponsored by loose-knit associations or societies sometimes called clans, although membership in these organizations bears little relation to the Hidatsa's traditional clans.

Sponsoring a powwow is costly. The sponsor gives bread, coffee, meat, canned fruit, and other food to each family that camps at the powwow grounds. The outdoor powwows involve Indian dance contests. The people compete in different categories of dances and the winners receive cash prizes. The dance drummers and singers are paid for their work.

The associations work all winter at fund-raising activities for the powwow.

Summer powwows are held outdoors at various locations on the reservation. Indians, who come from all over to attend these events, camp in trailers or temporary shelters for the duration of the powwow, which involves several days of dancing, eating, and socializing.

Families are expected to aid relatives in raising the money for the powwow, a carryover from the old days when everyone contributed to the welfare of the tribe. One popular way of raising money is to hold bingo games. The association women sell raffle tickets and refreshments at these games and auction off food, quilts, and other items to add to the proceeds. Some associations also hold special fund-raising events called War Bonnet ceremonies. The families of the officers of the association contribute war bonnets made for this purpose, quilts, shawls, and other items to be auctioned off to raise funds.

In addition to powwows, giveaway ceremonies are uniquely Indian. Giveaways are held to mark special occasions, such as receiving an Indian name, graduating from school, leaving for military service, retiring, being elected to tribal office, or receiving a special honor. Based on the traditional Indian principle that no one achieves anything without help, the family of the

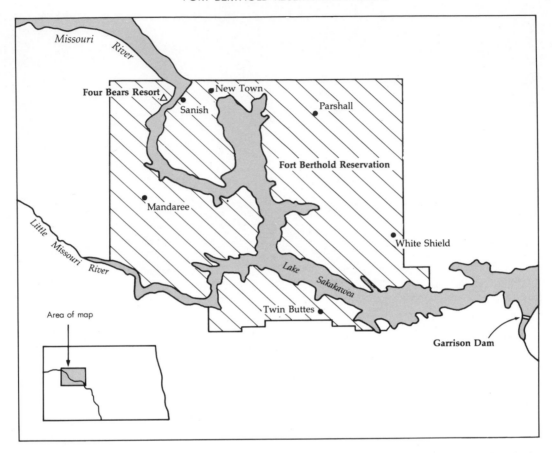

honoree gives away quilts, blankets, shawls, yard goods, and other items to friends who have in some way helped the person. People who receive gifts on behalf of a child are obligated to help the youngster throughout his or her life. Prosperous families give gifts to strangers so that word of the tribe's hospitality will spread to other tribes.

Employment differences exist between Indians and non-Indians on Fort Berthold Reservation. Most non-Indians are ranchers or farmers, but only a small proportion of Indians make their living this way. The majority of Indians are employed in government jobs as there is not much industry in rural North Dakota. The largest employer on the reservation is the federal government. Many Indians work for the Bureau of Indian Affairs or the Indian Health Service. The tribal government also employs a number of people. Indians who teach in public schools on the reservation are employed by the local government.

The legal battles over Garrison Dam gave the tribal leaders experience that they are using to strengthen the tribe's political powers. In 1970 the Department of the Interior ruled that the opening of the reservation to non-Indian settlement in 1910 had not removed any land from the reservation; the boundaries continued to be those established in 1886. On the basis of this legal opinion, New Town, Parshall, and other mainly non-Indian communities were found to be within the boundaries of the reservation. The non-Indian landowners were unhappy with the change, but the tribe considered it a major legal victory. After years in which land had been lost, an area amounting to more than one-quarter the size of the entire reservation had been returned.

The restoration of land to Fort Berthold Reservation led to problems between the Indians and non-Indians living within its newly determined boundaries. As independent sovereign nations governed by their own constitutions, incorporated Indian tribes have the right to make and enforce their own laws. It is this right, known as jurisdiction, that has created controversy on reservations. Indians and non-Indians disagree whether tribal laws apply to all people living on reservations or whether they apply to Indians only. If, for example, a tribe passes a law restricting the sale or consumption of alcoholic beverages, must non-Indians obey it? Can the tribe arrest a non-Indian who breaks tribal law?

The issue of jurisdiction at Fort Berthold was even more confusing because the land sold under the agreement of 1910 was removed from the reservation at that time. The non-Indians who bought this land at that time never lived on the reservation. When the land was returned to the reservation in 1970, they came under Indian jurisdiction. The non-Indians felt that their rights were being violated and protested to their representatives in Congress. No decision concerning jurisdiction has been reached, and the issue continues to be vigorously debated by Indians and non-Indians.

The division of allotments among the heirs of original allottees continues to cause problems among the Hidatsa today. Often the several heirs to an allotment do not agree on whether the land should be kept in the family or sold, and legal battles ensue over what should be done with it. When heirs agree to sell the land, the proceeds are divided among them. When they cannot agree, the tribe assumes control of the property and leases the land until the issue is settled in court. In the meantime, any income from rent is divided among the heirs. Many Indians who own fractions of allotments lease the property to non-Indians because their portion of the land is too small to be used for farming or grazing cattle. Often the quarterly lease checks that a person receives for leasing the land are too little to affect a family's economic situation.

A new generation of Hidatsa has reached adulthood since the construction of Garrison Dam. These contemporary descendants of the People of the Willows, though thoroughly integrated into modern American society, are just as interested as their ancestors were in preserving their cultural heritage.

In 1987 the Three Affiliated Tribes won the right to sue non-Indians in state court. The Indians wanted to sue Wold Engineering for faulty installation of water pipes on the reservation, but the company would not agree to be sued in the tribal court. The tribe then petitioned for the case to be heard in state district court. The district judge refused to try the case. The Indians appealed to the North Dakota Supreme Court, which upheld the district court's decision. Then the Indians took the case to the United States Supreme Court and eventually won the right to try the case in the North Dakota state court system. The tribe's success in this case established a precedent for other North Dakota tribes. In another legal action the tribe regained the mineral rights to lands flooded by the reservoir.

Now the Three Tribes are seeking additional compensation for the damage done by Garrison Dam. They charge that the flooding of their land destroyed their self-sufficient way of life. A committee appointed by the secretary of the interior in 1986 to study the Indians' claim agreed, recommending that the Three Tribes receive between $178 and $412 million as compensation for the loss of land and resources. Although no bill to carry out this decision has been introduced in Congress, the Three Tribes are hopeful that their representatives will sponsor such legislation soon. The Indians propose that the settlement money be derived from electric power revenues generated by federally operated dams, including Garrison Dam. In addition to the claims payment, they are also asking that money be set aside for water projects on the reservation, and for authorization for the construction of replacements for the hospital and other facilities that were destroyed by Lake Sakakawea.

A new generation has grown up since the move out of the valley. This new generation has more formal education, but it is also concerned with maintaining traditional customs and ideals. New federal policies support the teaching of Indian languages and allow the revival of traditional religious practices. These encourage young people to learn about their heritage and their elders to practice and teach it. There is good reason to believe that the new generation of Hidatsa, Mandan, and Arikara is regaining the sense of community and purpose that motivated their ancestors' lives. ▲

BIBLIOGRAPHY

Bodmer, Karl. *Karl Bodmer's America*. Edited by David Hunt and Marsha V. Gallagher. Lincoln: University of Nebraska Press, 1984.

Boller, Henry. *Among the Indians: Four Years on the Upper Missouri, 1858–1862*. Lincoln: University of Nebraska Press, 1972.

Bowers, Alfred. *Hidatsa Social and Ceremonial Organization*. Washington, D.C.: Government Printing Office, 1964.

Case, Harold W. *100 Years at Ft. Berthold*. Bismarck (North Dakota) Tribune, 1976.

Catlin, George. *Letters and Notes on the Manners, Customs, and Conditions of North American Indians*, vol. 1. 1844. Reprint. New York: Dover Publications, 1973.

Gilman, Carolyn, and Mary Jane Schneider. *The Way to Independence: Memories of a Hidatsa Indian Family*. St. Paul: Minnesota Historical Society, 1987.

Meyer, Roy. *The Village Indians of the Upper Missouri*. Lincoln: University of Nebraska Press, 1977.

Wilson, Gilbert L. *Agriculture of the Hidatsa Indians*. Minneapolis: University of Minnesota Studies in Social Science, 1917.

————. *Goodbird, the Indian*. St. Paul: Minnesota Historical Society, 1984.

————. *The Hidatsa Earthlodge*. Anthropology Papers of the American Museum of Natural History, vol. 33. pt. 5. New York, 1934.

————. *Waheenee*. Lincoln: University of Nebraska Press, 1984.

THE HIDATSA AT A GLANCE

TRIBE *Hidatsa*

CULTURE AREA *Northern Plains*

GEOGRAPHY *Missouri River basin and western Plains*

LINGUISTIC FAMILY *Siouan*

CURRENT POPULATION *combined membership of the Three Affiliated Tribes: 6,897*

FIRST CONTACT *La Vérendrye, French, 1738*

FEDERAL STATUS *recognized. In 1934 the Hidatsa, Mandan, and Arikara adopted a tribal constitution and incorporated as the Three Affiliated Tribes.*

GLOSSARY

acculturation The process by which one culture changes and adapts to the dominant culture it confronts.

agent; Indian agent A person appointed by the Bureau of Indian Affairs to supervise U.S. government programs on a reservation and/or in a specific region; after 1908 the title "superintendent" replaced "agent."

allotment U.S. policy, applied nationwide since 1887, to break up tribally owned reservations by assigning individual farms and ranches to Indians. Intended as much to discourage traditional communal activities as to encourage private farming and assimilate Indians into mainstream American life.

annuity Compensation for land and/or resources based on terms of a treaty or other agreement between the United States and an individual tribe; consisted of goods, services, and cash given to the tribe every year for a specified period.

Archaic Period The time when people in North America began using a variety of stone and bone tools and got food by hunting and gathering. It was generally characterized by seasonal migrations and the use of fire and showed effective use of local natural resources. For the Plains Indians, the Archaic Period was from about 8,000 to 2,000 years ago.

Awatixa One of three related groups of people that lived along the Missouri River and became part of the Hidatsa tribe; the village inhabited by these people.

Awaxawi One of three related groups of people that lived along the Missouri River and became part of the Hidatsa tribe; the village inhabited by these people.

B.P. Before the present.

Beringia The land bridge over which human beings crossed from Asia to North America more than 14,000 years ago.

Bureau of Indian Affairs (BIA) A U.S. government agency established in 1824 and assigned to the Department of the Interior in 1849. Originally intended to manage trade and other relations with Indians, the BIA is now involved in developing and carrying out programs to encourage Indians to manage their own affairs and to improve their educational opportunities and general social and economic well-being.

clan A multigenerational group having a shared identity, organization, and property, based on belief in descent from a common ancestor. Because clan members consider themselves closely related, marriage within the clan is strictly prohibited. Hidatsa clan membership is passed through the mother's family.

council of elders A group of men, selected from among the heads of families, that governed each village and made community decisions.

creation or **origin myth** A sacred narrative that the people of a society believe explains the origins of the world, their own institutions, and their distinctive culture.

culture The learned behavior of human beings; nonbiological, socially taught activities; the way of life of a given group of people.

Folsom culture A way of life during the late Paleo-Indian Period (about 10,000 years ago), named for the New Mexico town near which a distinctive projectile point of this culture was first discovered.

fractionated heirship The division of an allotment among a number of heirs into plots of land that are often too small to be economically useful.

General Allotment Act An 1887 law requiring that tribally owned reservation lands be subdivided into plots given, or allotted, to individual Indians. It was intended to speed the assimilation of Indians into the mainstream of American life by turning them into farmers.

giveaway A tradition of personal sacrifice and sharing to which federal officials and missionaries objected because it undermined adjustment to practices of free enterprise and personal saving.

Hidatsa An Indian tribe of the northern Great Plains; one of three original groups of people that lived along the Missouri River and became part of the Hidatsa tribe; the village inhabited by these people.

horticulture Production of food using human muscle power and simple hand tools to plant and harvest domesticated crops.

Indian Reorganization Act The 1934 federal law that ended the policy of allotting plots of land to individuals and provided for political and economic development of reservation communities.

matrilocal residence A tradition in which a newly married couple lives with or near the wife's mother's family.

Naxpike or *Hidebeating Ceremony* or *Sun Dance* A sacred ceremony involving chanting, personal sacrifice, and feasting, widely observed by Plains Indians.

Paleo-Indian Period The period in North America lasting until about 10,000 years ago when the way of life of humans involved hunting large mammals and making specialized stone tools.

polygyny A form of marriage in which a man may have two or more wives at the same time.

powwow An Indian social gathering that includes feasting, dancing, rituals, and arts and crafts displays, to which other Indian groups as well as non-Indians are now often invited.

projectile points Weapon tips made of stone and attached to wooden shafts to produce spears or lances. The Paleo-Indians produced unique fluted points.

reservation or *reserve* A tract of land set aside by the U.S. or Canadian government specifically for occupation and use by Indians.

sacred bundle A collection of objects believed to have spiritual powers and used in various rituals.

Three Affiliated Tribes A federally recognized tribe made up of Hidatsa, Mandan, and Arikara Indians; incorporated in 1934 and governed by a tribal constitution.

treaty A contract negotiated between representatives of the United States or another national government and one or more Indian tribes. Treaties dealt with surrender of political independence, peaceful relations, land sales, boundaries, and related matters.

tribe A type of society consisting of several or many separate communities united by kinship, a common culture, language, and such social units as clans, religious organizations, and economic and political institutions. Tribes are generally characterized by economic and political equality and thus lack social classes and authoritative chiefs.

Winters Doctrine The legal right of Indian tribes to use water that flows through their reservations for irrigation purposes; the result of the 1908 Supreme Court decision *Winters v. United States*.

Woodland Period The time when people in North America practiced horticulture, made pottery, used the bow and arrow, buried their dead in cemeteries marked by mounds of earth, and lived in permanent villages. For the Plains Indians, the Woodland Period was from about 2,000 to 1,200 years ago.

PICTURE CREDITS

MARY JANE SCHNEIDER is professor of Indian studies at the University of North Dakota. She received her M.A. and Ph.D. in anthropology from the University of Missouri. She has published numerous papers in professional journals on Plains Indian art, beadwork, basketry, and women's work. *The Way to Independence*, a book that she coauthored with Carolyn Gilman, was published by the Minnesota Historical Society to accompany an exhibition on the Hidatsa. In connection with the centennial of North Dakota's statehood in 1989, she is writing a book on the history and culture of the native peoples of North Dakota.

FRANK W. PORTER III, general editor of INDIANS OF NORTH AMERICA, is director of the Chelsea House Foundation for American Indian Studies. He holds a B.A., M.A., and Ph.D. from the University of Maryland. He has done extensive research concerning the Indians of Maryland and Delaware and is the author of numerous articles on their history, archaeology, geography, and ethnography. He was formerly director of the Maryland Commission on Indian Affairs and American Indian Research and Resource Institute, Gettysburg, Pennsylvania, and he has received grants from the Delaware Humanities Forum, the Maryland Committee for the Humanities, the Ford Foundation, and the National Endowment for the Humanities, among others. Dr. Porter is the author of *The Bureau of Indian Affairs* in the Chelsea House KNOW YOUR GOVERNMENT series.